HAUNTING FIRESIDE STORIES

by A.S. Mott

Ghost House Books

First printed in 2005 10 9 8 7 6 5 4 3 2 1
Printed in Canada

The Publisher: Ghost House Books
Distributed by Lone Pine Publishing
10145 – 81 Avenue
Edmonton, AB T6E 1W9
Canada

1808 – B Street NW, Suite 140
Auburn, WA 98001
USA

Website: http://www.ghostbooks.net

Library and Archives Canada Cataloguing in Publication

Mott, A.S. (Allan S.), 1975-
Haunting Fireside Stories / by A.S. Mott.

ISBN 1-894877-55-1

Ghosts. 2. Tales. I. Title.

GR580.M682 2005 398.25 C2005-902337-6

Editorial Director: Nancy Foulds
Project Editors: Carol Woo, Rachelle Delaney
Illustrations Coordinator: Carol Woo
Production Manager: Gene Longson
Book Design, Layout & Production: Curtis Pillipow, Heather Markham
Cover Design: Gerry Dotto

Photo credits: Every effort has been made to accurately credit photographers. Any errors or omissions should be directed to the publisher for changes in future editions. The photographs in this book are reproduced with the kind permission of the following sources: Dwight Allott (p. 99); Istock (p. 15: Jan Abt; p. 59: Greg Nicholas; p. 110: Jessica Jones; p. 136: Amanda Rohde; p. 146: Nathan Goodman; p. 164: Jan Ball; p. 168: Matthew Dula)

We acknowledge the financial support of the Government of Canada through the Book Publishing Industry Development Program (BPIDP) for our publishing activities.

PC: P5

To Lynne Zenko
The Most Popular Person I Know

Contents

Acknowledgments

I would like to thank my mother, Wendy Mott and my aunt, Lynne Zenko for being as good and kind and wonderful as any two human beings have any right to be. I feel like I've won the lottery to be lucky enough to be related to both of them.

I also would like to thank Carol Woo, my editor, for not hitting me when most people would consider physical violence to be completely justified, as well as Rachelle Delaney who provided notes that proved invaluable. I also must thank Nancy Foulds, Shane Kennedy and my heart knows nothing but gratitude for the fine work of Curt Pillopow.

Both Dan Asfar and Shelagh Kubish have earned my thanks for kindly responding to several e-mails I sent to them in moments of panic. My incredible Marketing Posse forever deserve my respect and admiration for putting up with my less-admirable authorial antics (as well as for unknowingly supplying me with several names in *Samantha's Diary* when I needed them).

But most of all I want to thank you, the reader, because without you I'm just a guy who spends way too much time sitting at his computer, typing far too fast to spell even the simplest words the same way they appear in your more conventional dictionaries. Tank u.

Introduction

One of the most frustrating challenges I face as a writer of ghost stories is the perception among many readers that a story about the supernatural should invariably be a chilling tale of terror. Scary stories can be a lot of fun to write, but my favorites are often the ones that use the idea of life after death as a catalyst for something more than straight-ahead horror. Not only does it make my job more interesting, but by being willing to explore the worlds of comedy, romance and drama in a paranormal setting, it allows me to create narratives that are far more unpredictable than the same-old, same-old. This collection of five stories represents my attempt to take the ghost story and explore it to the fullest.

The first story, *Happily Ever Hereafter*, is my own tribute to those wild and zany romantic comedies that flew so effortlessly off of P.G. Wodehouse's typewriter. Its genesis begin with a phone call I shared with my fellow Ghost House author Dan Asfar, where I explained how I enjoyed sometimes starting a story without knowing anything about it. "For example," I told him, "I'll just start a story with a woman crying alone in a restaurant and see where it takes me from there." To prove my point, I sat down after the call ended and wrote *Happily Ever Hereafter*'s first paragraph and was delighted to discover what happened after that in much the same way you should.

With *The Hunt*, the book's second story, I had a much better idea of what was going to happen in it when I started it, but I found that it was easily as much fun to write as *Happily Ever Hereafter*. Clearly my inspiration here was John Landis' classic movie *An American Werewolf in London*, but more in the way that film cleverly combines humor with horror than simply the fact that both are about werewolves.

When I finished writing the book's third story, *The Living Dead*, I had no idea how controversial its subject matter would prove to be by the time it was actually published. It was almost eerie how relevant this story became, given the recent issues over the life of a terminally ill woman in Florida. And lest you think that in it I am espousing one particular point of view regarding its subject matter, I suggest you read it again and see that the conclusions I reach are much more complicated than they would first appear.

The book's fourth story, *Samantha's Diary*, just might be my favorite out of all the ones I have ever written up to this time. Like *Happily Ever Hereafter*, I started it without knowing anything about its characters or eventual plot. All I knew was that I wanted to tell a story in diary form from the point of view of a recently deceased individual. I don't know why I made this person a teenaged girl or why I set the story in its specific time frame, but I am very happy that I did. As I was writing the story I suddenly realized where it was inevitably heading and the thought of it scared me a lot, but once I got there I realized that it was the only place this story could have ever gone. I hope you like it even half as much as I do.

I originally wrote *Reality Television*, the book's last story, for *Fireside Ghost Stories*, but when space limitations required me to cut one story out of the text, it was the one I chose to go. This decision had nothing to do with its quality, but rather my feeling at the time that it was unfinished and lacked a proper ending. This book has given me a chance to work on the story some more and add all of the elements I felt it had been missing in its original incarnation. Of all the stories in this book, it is easily the most conventionally scary, but I don't mind that so much, since I was also able to weave in a layer of gentle satire throughout its various horrific tableaus.

Happily Ever Hereafter

It was hard for the other diners not to notice Angelina as she sat alone at her table in the dark corner of the restaurant. She was a very striking woman whose beauty frequently attracted the attention of those around her. But that wasn't why everyone at the restaurant was glancing over in her direction. No, everyone at the restaurant was keenly aware of her presence tonight because she was crying. Loudly. To the point of wailing. The restaurant was very hip and exclusive, and many of the people eating there had waited for months to get a table. The last thing they wanted to deal with as they ate was the despairing sobs of an obviously upset woman (no matter how fetching she looked in her evening dress).

As she cried, Angelina looked up and noticed everyone staring at her. She cried even harder, knowing now that she was turning into an unpleasant curiosity. She jumped up from her chair, grabbed her purse and ran across the restaurant into the women's bathroom. The trio of young trophy wives chatting cattily in front of the bathroom mirror dispersed as soon as they saw that the woman they were talking about had just joined them. They left her alone and she stood and sobbed in front of the mirror. She looked up as she cried and caught sight of herself in the mirror. Her face was splotchy and red, and black mascara streaked her entire face. Her nose was runny and her hair was in complete disarray. She looked like a horrible monster. If she was in a 50s B-movie, they would call her the Colossal Hysterical Woman.

She had to calm down. She stopped crying and wiped her nose. Then she cleaned up her face, redid her makeup and fixed up her hair. Her eyes were still puffy and her face was still red, but she no longer looked crazy or upset. She walked out the bathroom and went back to her table. All eyes followed her as she made the trip, but she ignored them. She had come to this restaurant for a reason and she wasn't about to let other people's reactions to her distress get in her way.

She was there to honor Cal and that was all that mattered.

Cal had been her husband. He had died in a water-skiing accident eight months ago; when he and some friends were attempting to build a human pyramid, a lone seagull got in his way and slammed into his nose. The impact caused the pyramid to topple and knocked him unconscious. Too strong a swimmer to bother wearing a life jacket, he sank into the water and by the time his dazed friends had enough sense to realize he wasn't with them, he had drowned.

It was a senseless death made all the more horrible by his youth—he was only 32—and because the whole incident was videotaped by another vacationer who sent it in to a TV show and won $10,000 for that week's funniest clip. Wacky sound effects were added to the image and the host didn't mention to the people watching at home that one of the skiers had died. Everyone told Angelina that she should sue the show's producers, but she was far too overcome with grief to even think about going to court. Plus it wasn't as though she needed the money.

Despite Cal's youth, he had left his widow a fortune. He had gotten into and out of the Internet tech boom at just the right time. Thanks to his investment in a web site that sold beachwear and tanning supplies, he got both a million-dollar bank account and a gorgeous young wife, whom he met when she was hired to model bikinis for the web site.

The first time Angelina saw him, she was trying to pull off the difficult trick of looking sexy while lying on a cold beach in frigid water. He was tanned and athletic, and she was shocked to learn that he was the guy signing her paycheck. He looked more like a surfer than a young entrepreneur. She, on the other hand, looked exactly how a bikini model should look and Cal was instantly smitten. The two of them dated for two weeks before it became evident that they were soul mates and destined to spend the rest of their lives together. They got married on the beach and lived happily for six years. During that time Cal sold his stock in the web site when it was still worth something, and used the money to start a surfboard company. The day he died, his company was worth $10,000,000.

That figure meant little to Angelina as she sat back down at her table. She would happily give it all away to share even one more minute with him if she could. Instead, the best she could do was wear the dress he always loved to see her in, go to his favorite restaurant and celebrate what would have been their seventh wedding anniversary. Determined not to break down again, she caught the attention of her waiter—who had avoided her like she was radioactive just a few minutes earlier—and asked for a glass of champagne and the house salad (grieving widow or not, she was still watching her weight). She ate and drank with as much dignity as she could while people continued to stare at her.

She knew they could never understand her pain. A love like the one she and Cal had shared was one in a million, and she doubted there was anyone in this whole shallow, heartless city who knew its equal. She finished her meal and closed her eyes, remembering how Cal had looked the night he had sat across from her at that very table. She fought against her urge to weep again, and instead she stood up, paid the check and walked out of the restaurant with her head held high.

The restaurant's front entrance was crowded with people waiting to get in. Excited paparazzi buzzed about the possibility that Declan McGregson—the young new Irish superstar—might be eating there that night. Angelina walked passed them, causing a few flashbulbs to go off before the photographers realized that the beautiful woman walking past them wasn't anyone famous. She didn't even notice they were there. She walked over to one of the parking valets and handed him her ticket. He nodded and went to retrieve her car. It was cold out, and a light drizzle began to fall. It felt good against her exposed skin and she made no attempt to move away from the curb as it fell. She looked up into the dark night air and imagined Cal as an angel living in the clouds up above her.

This thought made her smile and she closed her eyes. From behind her she heard shouting, but she did not hear what was said. Then, in front of her, she heard the sound of a loud roaring engine. She opened her eyes just in time to see a black luxury sedan speeding towards her. Before she could think to react in any way, the car slammed into her and sent her flying into the air. Her thoughts went black and her body fell back down to the cold, wet ground.

* * *

She saw a bright light. Actually, she saw a lot of bright lights. The flashes of the photographers' cameras popped incessantly as the men and women who held them literally fought to get unobstructed shots of what would undoubtedly be the biggest scandal of the year—if not the decade. Declan

McGregson, the handsome king of the action picture, had just—before their very eyes—run over a beautiful young woman who had been standing outside one of the city's most exclusive restaurants. Punches were thrown as they all tried to get a good picture of an obviously intoxicated McGregson. But who was the victim?

"She looks like she was a model," one of them shouted out to a colleague as he aimed his camera.

"Yeah," his colleague agreed. "It's too bad. Imagine how this would play if she was a grandmother or something?"

His buddy laughed at this.

"This is L.A., man," he reminded the guy, "for all we know she's 62 and a grandmother of five."

Angelina was appalled by this conversation.

"There is no way I could ever be that old!" she insisted, but the two guys didn't hear her. No one seemed to hear her. She knew they couldn't hear her, but that didn't stop them from seeming rude.

She had died the instant the car hit her body. Her spirit had remained standing at the curb while her body was propelled into the air. Her first thought, as the car drove through her spiritual essence, was *Ohmygod, was that Declan McGregson*? Her second was an oath of profanity aimed at the young actor's direction, and her third was a simple *what happens now*? The proper responses to these thoughts were, in order, 1) yes, 2) that's not physically possible and 3) a tired-looking guy in a white suit shows up.

The guy in the white suit was late, so Angelina was forced to wait around while the police came and the photographers went berserk. They all knew that they could retire from the money these pictures were going to make them. As the minutes

passed, her spirit moved around the crowd in a way that wasn't like walking, but felt too earthbound to be called floating. She listened to McGregson as he wept over what he had done and she stood in front of the paparazzi's camera's in the hope that the shots would be ruined by whatever it was that made pictures blurry when people took photographs of ghosts.

A whole hour passed. Finally, a guy in a white suit showed up. He looked annoyed and was clearly unhappy about being late. From the way he moved towards her, she could tell that there was something unearthly about him. Or maybe it was just because he could see her when no one else could.

"I'm sorry," he spoke with an accent that sounded like a bad American actor attempting to imitate a wealthy Englishman, "but my last appointment proved far more stubborn than I expected."

"It's okay," she shrugged. "I didn't even know you were coming."

"Still," he insisted, "there is no excuse for being late. Especially in my profession."

"Which is?" Angelina asked.

"Oh, I'm sorry," he apologized before reaching into his jacket for a card, which he handed to her. It read:

MAURICE BIGGENS, ESQ.
Angel of Death

"So I'm definitely dead?" she asked him after she had looked at it.

"Definitely and without question," he said. "I'm afraid the damage the vehicle has done to your body is such that only an unqualified miracle could bring you back and we only allow for those on very special occasions."

"Gotcha," she said, taking this information in. She didn't feel at all like she had expected. She wasn't sad or anything. It had all happened so fast that it didn't even feel real. Maybe she would feel more passionately about it tomorrow when she had time to dwell on it. But the experience became overwhelming once she realized that she was dead, just like Cal. That meant a reunion with her beloved was only a short time away! All at once she felt her spirit tingle with an electricity that caused the hair of the living people all around her to stand up on end.

"Where's my husband, Maurice?" she asked. "Where is he? We have to be together!"

"First off," Maurice informed her, "it's pronounced Morris—you Americans always get that wrong—and secondly, I have to inform you of what your choices are before I can take you anywhere."

"I want to be with Cal," she insisted.

"Please, Mrs. Weathers. I have to do it properly or I might as well not do it at all."

"Fine." Angelina rolled her eyes. "Whatever. Just get on with it."

Maurice was losing his patience.

"I'm more than happy to, now that you have given me the chance," he said before he allowed himself a moment to center his *chi* and regain his composure.

"Come on!" she shouted at him.

"Fine!" he shouted back, his voice losing all trace of the English accent. "You're dead, right? Got that?"

"Yes!"

"Okay, so normally I'd just take you to the big hall of judgment in the sky and there you'd get judged on how much good you've done during the time allotted to you and you either get sent to Happyland or Losertown, depending on how you did, but in cases like yours we have to give you another option."

"What do you mean cases like mine?" she asked him.

"Sometimes an accident takes someone out of the game before their allotted time is up. Usually when that happens we just bung them back into their old body and they spend the rest of their lives boring people at cocktail parties about their out-of-body experiences, but—like I said earlier—we can't do that with you because your body is not retrievable. That means that I can either take you up to the J.P. where you'll get a more lenient judgment based on your shortened time on Earth or you can spend the next 43 years—the time you have remaining—here as a spirit amongst the living."

"A spirit? You mean a ghost?"

"I was under the impression that they meant the same thing, but yes, if that is how you want to put it."

Angelina worked to put this all together in her mind.

"So let me get this straight," she spoke aloud. "I can either go with you and get judged or stay here for awhile and then get judged?"

"Yes."

"And there's no way to avoid this whole judgment thingee?"

"No."

"Okay," Angelina nodded. "I want to be with Cal," she decided. "Where is he? Happyland, right? There's no way they would send him to Losertown."

"Why do you people always assume we know what happened to the people from your past? We handle thousands of people a day and it's not like many of you are at all memorable. I have no clue where this Cal guy is."

"Can't you find out? There must be records somewhere," Angelina pleaded.

Maurice let out a long painful sigh.

"Why do I always get the difficult ones?" he muttered to himself as he pulled out what looked like a cell phone, only it glowed and had no buttons on it. He flipped it open and spoke into it. "Hi Doris, it's Maurice." He paused for a second to grimace over the inadvertent rhyme. "I need you to pull a record for me...Yeah–huh...North American...I don't know. Let me ask." He cupped his hand over the phone's receiver and coughed to get Angelina's attention.

"Did he have the same last name as you?"

"Yes."

"Was he from L.A.?"

She nodded again.

He took his hand off of the receiver. "Yeah, he's a guy named Cal Weathers from L.A." He looked over at Angelina. "Something tells me he was either really rich or handsome. Probably both. Okay, no problem." He cupped his hand over the receiver again. "It'll be a minute," he informed Angelina.

A long silence passed as the two waited for Doris to come back with the information Maurice requested. During the uncomfortably quiet moment, they watched as the paparazzi went wild when Declan took a swing at one of the cops and was rewarded with a taser shot in the gut for his efforts.

"Yeah? You got it?" Maurice spoke when Doris finally picked up the phone. "So where is he?… Uh–huh… Yeah… Really? Are you sure?" He nodded and thanked Doris before he hung up and put the heavenly cell phone back into his jacket pocket.

"So where is he?" Angelina asked him impatiently.

Maurice paused uncomfortably and scratched the back of his neck. He hesitated.

"Aum…"

"Ohmygod!" Angelina read into his reluctance. "He is in Losertown!"

"No," Maurice shook his head. "He's not in Losertown."

"Thank God," she sighed with relief. "Then where is he?"

"It appears that when Cal died he faced the same situation you did. There was no way his spirit could be returned to his body and he still had 45 years allotted to him, so he decided to remain on the Earth as a spirit."

"You mean he's a ghost?"

"Yes." Maurice gritted his teeth. "That's what I said."

"Then where is he? Where is his ghost?"

"Well," Maurice explained, "most people, when they become spirits, choose to search out and stay with the person with whom they felt the closest bond during their life. That is what he did."

"But his closest bond was with me," Angelina insisted. "Does that mean his spirit has been with me all along? Is he here right now?" She turned her head to look for him. "Cal? Cal?" she shouted. "Where are you, sweetie?"

Maurice coughed uncomfortably and Angelina stopped.

"Do you know a woman named Cheryl Wilcox?" he asked.

Angelina thought it was strange that Maurice would bring her up.

"Yeah," she admitted with a confused look. "She and Cal used to go out in high school. She dumped him just before the senior prom. Why?"

Maurice managed to look even more uncomfortable than he already was. He raised his eyebrows and shrugged, hoping this would be enough to clue her in.

She looked at him with utter and complete disbelief.

"Carol Wilcox?" she shouted. "Carol Wilcox? He chose to search out and haunt Carol Wilcox?"

"It would appear so," Maurice nodded.

"That—" She then proceeded to call Cal a name so unpleasant it made Maurice wince.

"Is he with her right now?" she asked him as her venomous slur still lingered in the air.

"Yes."

"Haunting her? Like some protective invisible spirit?"

"That's right."

"That—" she then called him the same name as before, only louder and with a lot more passion.

"So I take it you no longer want to join him?" Maurice said.

"Are you kidding?" Angelina shouted. "You bet your ass I want to join him! You think I'm going to let him forget all about me and spend the next four decades watching his old girlfriend whenever she takes a shower? No way! He may not think we were soul mates now, but he will when I get through with him! Just you wait!"

Maurice sighed again and felt a sharp pain stir between his temples.

Why did he always get the difficult ones?

* * *

Cheryl felt ridiculous as she pretended to read a magazine while she sat impatiently in the grungy yellow waiting room. The blonde behind the desk—who had obviously been hired more for her measurements than her competence—continued to ignore her as she chatted away with an apparently equally vacuous friend on the phone.

"What am I doing here?" Cheryl muttered to herself as she turned the page of the magazine she was holding and came upon an article devoted to celebrities who had made the tragic mistake of being caught unattractive on camera. She put down the magazine and recalled the sign on the door of this office:

Damon Lee

Paranormal Investigator

Was she crazy? Who in their right mind would actually go to a place like this? A paranormal investigator? Why didn't he just call it like it is and say he's a Con Man Who Preys On Superstitious Idiots?

But despite her feelings of foolishness and skepticism, she stayed put and waited until Mr. Lee was ready to talk to her. She had no choice. Maybe she was crazy, but the shrink she was seeing hadn't been able to help her. And all the holy men she had talked to weren't any better. This Lee guy was her last resort and she prayed it wasn't a scam.

"Miss?" the blonde behind the desk called out.

"Yes?" Cheryl looked up.

"Mr. Lee can see you now."

Cheryl walked over to the door behind the blonde's desk and let herself in. The first thing she saw was a short pudgy man sitting behind a desk. His fine blonde hair was thinning and his waistline was not. He was dressed in a blue tracksuit, which was odd since it seemed unlikely that he had done any kind of running ever.

"Hello there, Miss Wilcox," he stood up and greeted her, the top of his head barely reaching her shoulders. "I'm sorry to keep you waiting, but I was dealing with another case."

"That's okay," she shrugged politely.

"Why don't you sit down and tell me why you're here." He pointed to the rickety-looking chair that sat in front of his desk.

She sat down uneasily, finding herself face-to-face with the strange little man. It occurred to her, looking at him, that if he had been a doctor or a lawyer she would have turned around and run out of the office the second she saw him, but as a paranormal investigator, his shabby appearance actually worked in his favor. If he had looked at all slick she would have known instantly that this was a sham and he was just after her money. Instead, he looked as detached from sartorial reality as she imagined a true believer of this sort of thing should look.

"So what brings you here?" he prodded her after a few seconds of uncomfortable silence.

Don'tsayitdon'tsayitdon'tsayitdon'tsayitdon'tsayit, her brain ordered her, just like it had every time she even considered telling someone about what was happening at her house. But this time she ignored it. If she couldn't tell Damon Lee, then there was nobody she could tell.

"I think my house is haunted," she blurted out as quickly as she could, her face instantly reddening the second the words were out of her mouth.

"I see," Damon nodded without judgment. "And what makes you think that?"

"I hear things. I see things. Sometimes I even think I feel things."

"Like what? Can you give me some examples?"

"I hear humming."

"Really? Any specific tune?"

"*All Out of Love* by Air Supply mostly."

Damon winced.

"You poor woman," he sympathized. "And what do you see?"

"Strange shadows. Objects moving one their own accord. The occasionally hazy mist."

"Uh–huh." Damon nodded as he wrote this down. "And what have you felt?"

Cheryl hesitated. The idea of what she was about to say struck her as so crazy she almost couldn't bear to let it out.

"A man's hands," she finally answered. "On my shoulders, giving me a massage."

"A massage?"

"Yeah," she nodded. "It was okay, I guess, but whoever it was obviously wasn't an expert or anything."

"Looks like a classic case of a lost love," Damon informed her.

"A what?"

"The humming of cheesy romantic music, the massage—it all adds up to this ghost being someone you were close to earlier in your life," he explained.

"An old boyfriend?"

"Exactly. Can you think of who that would be?"

"I don't know," she admitted.

Damon leaned in and asked. "There's been a lot of them?"

"No," she answered him with an annoyed expression on her face. "It's just that I've lost contact with most of them, so I have no idea if any of them have died. He would have to be dead, right?"

"That's how it usually works," Damon agreed. "In most cases like this, the spirit belongs to a person who died during the relationship. I take it that isn't the case here?"

"That's right," she nodded. "I've never had a guy die on me before I broke up with him."

Damon started to write this down, but then her words made him pause.

"Before you broke up with them?" he asked.

"Yes."

"Have you been the person who ended all of your relationships?"

"Yes."

"You've never been dumped?"

She shrugged." I just have a knack for knowing when it's time to see other people," she told him.

"Okay," he mumbled as he jotted this down.

"What's that supposed to mean?"

"Nothing." He shook his head as he looked down at his notes. "Just seems a little cold is all," he mumbled under his breath.

"Excuse me?"

"It was nothing," he insisted. "Now, were any of these guys really sad to see you go?"

She thought for a second. "Pretty much all of them," she admitted.

"You must be a great catch," he mumbled again, but this time she caught what he said.

"Better than great," she agreed. "I'm amazing."

"Are you currently seeing someone?"

"No."

"Why not?"

"Work's been crazy," she told him. "Plus my house is haunted. Or did I already mentioned that?"

"How long has it been since you first noticed the presence of the spirit?"

"About eight months."

"Why did you wait so long before you sought the help of a paranormal professional?"

"Because I wanted to make sure I wasn't going crazy first."

"Well," he said, putting down his pen, "it's a good thing you finally came to me, and it's a very good thing that you haven't been dating since the ghost first appeared."

"Why is that?"

"Because, while this ghost is all Air Supply and massages right now, chances are if you did bring another man into the house, the spirit would stop being so friendly."

"You mean this thing could be dangerous?"

"As dangerous as any person consumed by jealousy."

"What can we do to get rid of it?"

"Before we can do anything, I have to make sure that everything I've just theorized is actually true. To do that I'll have to go to your house, but—for our safety—I'll go in disguised as a serviceman. Plus, I'll need you to write out a list of all your old boyfriends and their last known locations.

The quicker we figure out who this spirit is, the quicker we can deal with him."

"If it's so dangerous, should I stay at a hotel until you're finished?"

"No. The last thing we want to do is make it mad or arouse its suspicions. Until we know what to do, you should just act like everything is normal."

"Define normal."

"Just don't do anything to piss it off. There's nothing more potentially destructive than a lovesick spirit who's been rejected by the object of its affections."

"Nothing?"

"Nothing."

* * *

Cal was getting impatient. *Where was she?* Cheryl always came home from work at 5:45 PM. Her dependability that way was just one of the things he loved about her. *Maybe she got into an accident? Or maybe things are really piling up at the office and she had to stay late? Maybe she had to stop for groceries or went to grab some takeout.*

As he waited for her, he listed all of the possible reasons why she would be late getting home, except for one. And though he did not include it on his list, it was the one that worried him the most. It worried him so much he dared not even think it; lest his thoughts make it true.

What if she was out on a date? With another guy?

He knew he had no right to be jealous. She had dumped him over 16 years ago and was under no obligation at all to remain faithful to him or his memory (that is, if she were even aware that he was now a memory and not a living person).

It wasn't her fault that he had spent so much time imagining her in his daydreams, where he concocted scenarios where the two of them would accidentally run into each other and she would be instantly impressed by how handsome and how rich he had become. And it could have never occurred to her that when he died and he learned he had the option of staying on earth and being with the one person he truly cared about and that he chose her without even thinking about it. She probably hadn't thought about him in more than a decade! So any rational person, living or dead, could see that she was under no obligation to get home at 5:45 if she didn't want to, and as a single woman, she was well within her rights to go out and spend time with anyone she pleased.

Cal wanted to be rational. He really did. But there was something about Cheryl that just made a part of his brain stop working and so—even though he knew he had no right to be jealous—the thought of her out with another man was enough to make him want to break things.

He fought the urge to grab the object closest to him and hurl it against the wall. He counted to ten and did his best to calm down. He closed his eyes and tried to find his happy place. He found it and stayed there when he heard the sound of a key opening the front door. He breathed out a sigh of relief and waited for his true love to enter.

"How long is this going to take?" he heard her speak to someone behind her.

"An hour or two," a man answered her.

Out of instinct Cal's hand reached out to grab an ashtray, but he stopped when he saw that the man was dressed in a uniform of some kind. He wore a gray baseball cap that read *Moldbusters.*

"Is there any particular place you like to start looking for signs of the—uh—mold?" she asked the man.

"The living room is always the best place to start," the man answered.

"Okay. Can I get you a drink?"

"I'm good for now," said the man as he began pulling out some strange-looking instruments from his bag. One of the tools he pulled out was some sort of meter that began to beep as soon as its sensor hit the fresh air. "Yep," the man nodded as he looked at the small beeping box, "we definitely got some mold in here."

"Right here?" asked Cheryl. "In the living room?"

"Uh-huh."

"Is it—uh—enough that I should be worried?"

"I've seen worse," the man told her. "A lot worse. It won't take much to take care of this."

Cal felt relieved to hear that. He knew that Cheryl would probably have to leave the house if the mold problem was too much to take care of in a day or two. Plus he knew how expensive getting rid of that stuff could be, so it was good to know she wasn't about to get fleeced.

The mold man stayed for another hour as he went from room to room, performing his strange tests. Cal ignored him and spent the time with Cheryl, who stayed in the kitchen and made herself something to eat. She asked the mold man if he was hungry, but he declined—which was odd since he definitely looked like someone who loved food—and finished up. She was eating at the table when the man delivered his full report.

"You've definitely got some—uh—mold in the house, but it isn't a particularly strong one and I doubt that we'll have any problem getting it out of your hair. I just have to go back to my office and see if I can take that list you gave me and narrow it down to what specific—uh—mold it is."

"How long should this all take?"

"You should be completely mold free by the end of the week," he told her confidently.

"Thank God," she sighed.

Cal smiled, happy to see Cheryl happy, but his reverie was broken by the odd sight of a plate spinning directly toward his head. It spun right through him and crashed loudly against the kitchen wall behind him.

"What the hell was that?" Cheryl swore as she and the mold man quickly turned to see where the plate had been thrown.

Cal's eyes followed them. If ghosts could faint, he would have dropped to the ground right then and there.

"Angelina!" he shouted instead.

"YOU—" she swore angrily at him while she picked up another dish from the sink and heaved it toward him.

He ducked out of instinct, even though the plate would have passed through him again.

"What's going on?" Cheryl shouted to the mold man.

"I think the ghost is on to us," he answered.

Ghost? Cal paused. *I thought he was here for the mold?*

He didn't have much time to dwell on this with the sudden appearance of his beautiful widow.

"Angelina," he tried again. "What are you doing here?"

"What am I doing here?" she shouted. "What am I doing here?"

Her words were so shrill they broke past the barrier that separated the dead from the living. They were so loud that both Cheryl and Damon had to cover their ears to avoid being deafened by them.

Damon reacted by fumbling in his bag and pulling out the same meter he had used to spot Cal's presence in the kitchen. It began to beep so fast that it couldn't take the pace and exploded in Damon's hand.

"What does that mean?" Cheryl asked, sure she didn't want to know the answer.

"Things just got worse," Damon answered. "A lot worse."

* * *

Maurice had just dropped Angelina off and was on his way back to another difficult case when his cell phone rang. He moaned, knowing that these messages were never good.

"Hello?" he answered it.

"Maurice?" asked the voice on the other end. "Is that you?"

It was Leonard, the new guy.

"Yes," Maurice rolled his eyes. "Who else would it be?"

"Right, sorry," Leonard apologized.

"Is there anything I can do for you?" Maurice asked him impatiently.

"Yeah," said Leonard. "Have you gotten around to the Weathers case? The one in L.A.?"

"I just wrapped it up. Why?" Maurice asked, certain that the answer was going to be unpleasant.

"I kinda screwed up," said Leonard.

"What did you do?"

"When I was writing up her file I put a check beside 'Unrecoverable.'"

"And?"

"I shouldn't have. Turns out her body isn't damaged, so she can come back.."

"You're kidding me, right?"

"No."

Maurice sighed. "It's too late to do anything about it now," he insisted. "Her body has to be on its way to the morgue by now."

"It's at the hospital."

"Same thing. Either way, we don't have the time to get her back there before the autopsy, so she'll just have to stay a spirit until it's her time to go."

"It's not that simple," said Leonard.

Of course it wasn't. It never was. Maurice felt a migraine coming on.

"Why not?" he asked, as he stopped and pinched down on the bridge of his nose.

"She can't die. We have orders. *From the top*."

"From the top?"

"That's right."

"But why would the big guy care about a not-very-bright former swimsuit model?" Maurice wondered.

"It's not her," Leonard explained. "It's the movie star."

"Who?"

"Declan McGregson, the guy who ran into her. The big guy has big plans for him and apparently they don't involve vehicular manslaughter."

"Now you have to be kidding me, right?"

"No," insisted Leonard. "The accident was supposed to teach the two of them major lessons that they would use to rebuild their broken lives, but thanks to my screw up, she's dead and he's looking at serious jail time."

"So what are we supposed to do?"

"Well, I got the okay to grab a reserve spirit from the Limbo Division and put it into her body before they cut her up."

"Not bad. That way we have some time to get her back."

"Uh, not quite."

"Why not?"

"Well it turns out that at the hospital there is a nurse named Nona Tresario."

"So?"

"It seems that she's one of those...whatchamacallits... psycho stalker types. She's convinced that she and Declan are secretly married."

"Uh–huh?"

"So, when she finds out that Angelina is there, she's going to try and protect her man by dumping the body into the hospital's furnace and removing it as evidence of his crime."

"Of course she is. And when is this going to happen?"

"Two and a half hours from now."

"No problem." Maurice decided to be optimistic. "I'll just go to her spirit and get her to come back with me. It should take an hour tops."

"I hope so, man. Because the big guy has made it clear that unless we get this sorted out, he's going to be super pissed."

"So, situation normal," Maurice summed it all up before he hung up, turned around and headed back toward Angelina.

He hoped she wouldn't be unreasonable about all this.

* * *

"You're sitting on my hand," Damon complained to Cheryl.

"Tough," she whispered, "I couldn't move if I wanted to."

The two of them cowered in the tiny storage closet underneath Cheryl's stairway. It wasn't the perfect place to hide from the chaos that was currently running amok throughout her home, but it was the first one they found and they were going to stick with it.

They had initially tried to leave the house, but the front and back doors refused to open and some powerful force kept them from going out through any of the windows. They were trapped, and—for the moment—this tiny, uncomfortable spot was the safest place to be, unless you were Damon's right hand, which was—as he had complained—wedged underneath Cheryl's left buttock. But then, as much as it was beginning to hurt, he couldn't help but take some pleasure in his first real physical contact with a woman since his wife left him three years earlier.

"You are so pathetic," he cursed himself quietly.

"What was that?" she asked.

"Nothing," he insisted.

Cheryl winced as she heard the sound of another piece of furniture being destroyed outside the closet's door.

"Do you have insurance?" he asked.

"Yes," she answered. "But somehow I don't think I'm covered for acts of supernatural mayhem."

"You'd be surprised. Some of them big umbrella policies have clauses for just this very thing."

"Where? In Amityville?"

"Well, yeah," Damon admitted, "but in other places too."

"What happened? What made this guy go nuts?"

"I don't think it's him," Damon told her.

"What do you mean? Who else would it be?"

"I don't know, but before my meter exploded it was sensing the presence of so much spiritual energy there was no way it could come from just one ghost."

"So I got a duo in there?"

"Yeah."

"Fabulous," she moaned. "Maybe they'll invite their friends and have a real party."

* * *

Cal had so far failed to rein Angelina into a calm and rational discussion of the events. Instead he just stood and waited with his arms crossed as his wife demolished everything in the house that was the slightest bit demolishable. At first he had been stunned to see her in the kitchen, hurling plates and causing Cheryl and the mold guy to run for their lives. The last time he saw them they were attempting—to no avail—to throw a chair through the front window. The window was still there, so he assumed that they were either hiding or had found another way to escape from the house. Since then he had gone from amazement to confusion and was on his way to annoyance.

"Angelina!" he shouted impatiently as she started making blood drip down from the house's walls. "Enough is enough! Stop being so damn dramatic."

This caught her attention and finally made her stop. The blood stopped seeping out of the ceiling.

"You always have to be so theatrical!" he yelled. "You couldn't just say 'Hey buddy, you're a jerk for what you did.' No, you have to destroy a house. Typical."

She looked at him and took this in before she broke down sobbing.

Cal instantly felt guilty about what he had said. He rushed over and hugged her.

"I'm sorry,' he apologized. "I didn't mean it."

"Yes, you did," she wailed.

"No, I didn't," he insisted. "I was just mad, so I said the worse thing I could."

She cried some more, and he held her gently, waiting for her to become more rational and ready to talk.

"I'm sorry," she apologized when she was all cried out. "It's just you can't believe how bad I felt when that rude guy in the white suit told me where you had chosen to spend the rest of your time on earth."

"It must have been devastating," he agreed.

"I thought that we were soul mates and that you wanted to be with me more than anyone else in the world, and then I died and found out that I wasn't even close."

"That's not true," he said. "You were definitely first runner up. The silver medal for sure. And I can't even think of who the bronze would go to."

"That still makes me a loser." She started crying again.

"No it doesn't. You could never be a loser! Not with those legs."

A small smile appeared on her lips, but it quickly faded. "Then why did you pick Cheryl?" she asked.

He sighed and shrugged." She was the first," he told her. "And the first is always going to be remembered, no matter how bad it was." He paused and thought before he went on. "Cheryl was horrible to me. She treated me like dirt and got rid of me for a guy with a cooler car, but she was always the one I thought about. Can you imagine? There I was living with you—not only the most beautiful woman I had ever known, but also someone who truly and unconditionally loved me back—and I kept thinking about what my life would have been like if I had somehow made it work with Cheryl. It had nothing to do with you. I was just wondering what could have been. Everybody does that. I mean look at me! I had everything any man could want and I still did it. When I drowned and that nice woman in the white suit—"

"—You got a woman?" she interrupted, thinking of Maurice.

"Yeah." Cal nodded before he continued. "When that woman told me that I could go anywhere I wanted, I didn't choose you because that was where I had been. I wanted to see where I might have been. I convinced myself that I still loved Cheryl, but now that I think about it, I'm not sure I ever really did. I loved the idea of her."

He stopped and looked around the damaged remains of Cheryl's living room.

"You know," he began again, "now that you're here, I have to admit that she's not all that great. She's still really mean and shallow and I don't think she has any real friends." He thought for a moment and then his body tensed as if an important thought had just appeared fully formed in his mind. "You know how they say things happen for a reason?" he asked her when he was ready to let the thought be free.

"Yeah," she nodded.

"I think you've come to save me from my own blind stupidity. I was so enthralled by a vision of something that never was, I almost doomed myself to spending 45 years with someone I can't stand. I don't have to do that now. Instead I can spend the rest of the time I have here with the person I should have chosen in the first place."

Her face broke into a wide smile and she leaned forward and kissed him as hard as she could.

"Promise me we'll stay together," she whispered after the long kiss finally ended.

"I promise," he said as he ran his hand through her silky black phantom hair.

"Uh, excuse me," an uncomfortable voice coughed behind them.

They turned around and saw a tired-looking man in a white suit. Angelina recognized him. "Maurice, what do you want?"

"You," he answered. "I have to take you back."

* * *

Damon's hand was now numb. Visions of possible amputation came to his overactive imagination. He kept quiet about it, though. He didn't want Cheryl to think he was a wimp.

"It's been quiet for awhile now," he whispered to her. "Do you want to get out of here?"

"You're the expert," she answered him. "Do you think it's safe?"

"It could be," he said, "or this could just be the calm before a very bad storm."

"So we're staying, then," she decided.

"Have you been thinking about who these ghosts could be?" he asked her.

"Yeah, but it's not doing me any good. I still don't have any idea. And the more I try to think about who the first ghost could be, the more depressed I get."

"How come?"

"Because here I am making a list in my head of all these men I dated, and you know what? A lot of them were really cool guys who I could have had serious relationships with, but as soon as it got the slightest bit heavy, I just cut and ran. I did it every single time, right from the beginning with Cal Weathers to that guy named Operadude21 who I used to chat with on that singles web site."

"A lot of people do that." Damon tried to comfort her.

"Yeah, well, a lot of people are stupid, but that doesn't mean you should feel happy because you're one of them," she answered. "You know," she went on, "whoever this guy is—or was—he must be crazy."

"Why would you say that?"

"Because you said he came here because he loves me. That's nuts. Who in their right mind would love someone like me?"

Though he couldn't see her in the dark, Damon could tell that Cheryl was crying. He wanted to hug her, but his whole right arm was now numb and there wasn't enough room for him to do it with his left.

"I don't know," he said, "maybe someone who doesn't want a weak, easy-to-satisfy woman. A guy who likes a challenge. A man who actually deserves you and not some schmuck off the street. Why should you pick someone just because they might be right? You have every right to wait until you meet someone you know is the one you want. Anybody can find someone to be with, but it doesn't mean it's going to make them happy."

"Thanks," she sniffled in the darkness. "You know, for a guy with a really weird job, you sure do have your head on straight."

"I read a lot of self-help books," he admitted. "You'd be surprised by how much time I have off between cases."

* * *

"What do you mean?" asked Angelina.

"There's been a screw up," Maurice explained. "I have to take you back."

"I don't understand," said Cal. "Back to where?"

"To her body," answered Maurice. "She's not supposed to die."

"But you can't do that," she insisted. "Not when we just got back together."

"It's not up to me," Maurice told her. "This is an order from the highest power."

"So I have no choice?"

Maurice's headache went from bad to worse. She couldn't just come with him. No, she had to make it complicated and bring choice into the matter. For a second Maurice considered lying and telling her that she didn't have a choice and that his was the final word, but he knew that if there was an investigation into the incident and his deception was uncovered, there would be hell to pay.

"Yes, you have a choice," he sighed wearily. "I can't force you to come if you don't want to."

"Well, I don't want to," she said firmly.

"Honey," Cal looked into her eyes, "are you sure you don't want to live again?"

"That depends," she told him. "Can you bring Cal back too?" she asked Maurice.

"No," he answered her. "His body is long decomposed. There is nowhere for him to go."

"Then I'm staying here," she decided. "I'm not leaving Cal. Not again."

Maurice fought the urge to scream. "Are you crazy?" he shouted at her instead. "Do you know how many people get the second chance I'm giving you? And you're just going to let it pass you by so you can stay with the spirit of a guy who cheated on you by choosing to spend the rest of his time on earth haunting some bimbo who broke his heart in high school?"

"Yep," she answered without even thinking about it.

This time Maurice lost the fight and screamed out loud. "You stupid mortals!" he cursed them. "You can't let anything be easy, can you? You have to make everything so hard with your attachments and emotions!"

"Dude," said Cal, taken aback by the sudden outburst, "chill out."

Maurice calmed down instantly. "I'm sorry," he apologized, "but today has been a very tough day."

"That's okay," Cal shrugged. "Everybody gets stressed."

Maurice nodded at this sage wisdom and grabbed his cell phone from his jacket. He flipped it open, turned away from Angelina and Cal and called Leonard.

"Maurice," answered the new guy, whose voice had taken on the high-pitched timbre of extreme panic, "have you got the girl?"

"No," Maurice answered, causing Leonard to audibly deflate on the other end of the phone.

"It doesn't matter anyway," Leonard sighed pitifully, "not anymore."

"Why not?" asked Maurice.

"That stupid movie star, that's why. He took a swing at a cop and got a taser in his gut for the effort."

"Yeah, so?"

"So, he hit his head on the pavement when he fell and he just died 10 minutes ago from the trauma that resulted."

"You're kidding?"

"Does it sound like I'm kidding!" Leonard shouted.

"So just bung him back into his body," said Maurice. "Problem solved."

"He won't go back!"

"Why not?"

"Because he's crazy and wants to see his 'mum', who died when he was 12. I sent Janice over to deal with him, but even she can't convince him to get back into his body. We are so screwed here!"

"So where is he now?"

"He's at the same hospital where Angelina's body is being kept."

Maurice thought about this for a moment. "Are you sure he doesn't want to come back? Are you absolutely positive?" he asked.

"Yes."

"Okay," Maurice smiled. "I think I have a plan."

With that he hung up his phone and turned back to the reunited couple.

"Hey you two," he said. "I think we've found the solution to our little problem."

* * *

It was, by far, the biggest story of the year. Thanks to a combination of celebrity, glamor, a few miracles, redemption, forgiveness, dumb luck and a heavy dose of pure craziness, the public and the media—working in tandem—refused to let the story go and there wasn't a single person in the English-speaking world—including those who had spent the last 30 years living as hermits in the wilds of Montana—who didn't know what happened to Declan McGregson and Angelina Weathers.

Brought to the very depths of despair by the 15th anniversary of his beloved mother's death, the handsome Irish superstar drowned his sorrows in a bottle of whiskey before remembering he was to have dinner with his agent at a nearby restaurant. Far too drunk to drive, he got behind the wheel of his car anyway and drove erratically to the stylish eatery. At that moment, the beautiful Angelina—a former model and millionaire widow—was having her own breakdown inside that very restaurant. Later, while she waited for the parking valet to bring back her car, Declan lost complete control of his vehicle and drove into her, throwing her body 10 feet into the air.

This whole incident was recorded by the horde of photographers camped out in front of the restaurant waiting for Declan to appear. Based on the severity of the impact, everyone assumed that she was dead and little medical attention was given to her. Instead, they focused on the highly emotional actor who sobbed uncontrollably over what he had done and the still-painful memories of his mother's death. While he cried, one of the police officers made a comment about Declan's mother, which caused him to go insane with anger. He lunged at the officer and managed to punch him. Another officer grabbed a taser and shoved it into Declan's stomach, sending several thousand volts of electricity into his body. Declan collapsed and hit his head on the ground. Another ambulance was called and he was taken away to the hospital.

During this time, Angelina had been taken to the hospital, where she was written up as DOA. The first miracle occurred when an ER doctor detected that she still had a faint pulse. She was wheeled into a room and connected to a host of life support equipment, where she lingered in what everyone assumed was an irreversible coma. Then Declan's body came in, and—having no other place to put him—he was wheeled into the same room as his victim. By now he too had lapsed into a coma, and he flat-lined just a few minutes after he arrived at the hospital. The doctors attempted to revive him, but to no avail. His time of death was called at 8:25 PM.

The second miracle occurred when—15 minutes later—Declan awoke in his bed. To the amazement of the nurse—a Miss Nona Tresario—who had been in the room weeping over him, he sat up and looked over at the comatose beauty on a gurney to his right. He got up out of the bed and kissed her—much to the displeasure of Nurse Tresario whose screams brought other witnesses to the room. And there, in front of a group of disbelieving doctors, nurses and orderlies, Angelina awoke and kissed Declan back.

"I'm here, baby," Declan told her, his words sounding sweeter thanks to his charming brogue.

"I know you are, sweetie," she answered before they kissed again.

There was no explanation for it. Both of them had come back from beyond the veil of death and—despite never having previously met—instantly bonded in a passionate romance. She refused to press charges against him, and his lawyer was able to get his charges of resisting arrest and assaulting a police officer dismissed. Declan paid a $75,000 fine for drunk driving and was forced to serve 450 hours of community service.

He suffered amnesia from the head trauma, but it was a strange case in that only the details of his own life were affected. He could remember the president's name, but had no idea who his best friend or agent was. But it didn't take him long to relearn everything, and he and Angelina were married four months later.

During that time they both refused to be interviewed about what had happened to them, insisting that Declan was still dealing with his amnesia and Angelina was still healing from her physical injuries (which had proven to be less serious than anyone who saw the photos of her getting hit by the car would have assumed). Eventually, the couple had to give in to the intense and nonstop public interest, and they sat down for an exclusive interview with the host of television's top-rated news show.

When asked why he had kissed her after awaking from his coma, Declan just smiled and said, "Look at her. Wouldn't you?" And when she was asked how she could forgive him for what he had done to her, she just shrugged and said, "It was an accident. It wasn't like he wanted to hit me. And anyway, if he hadn't, I wouldn't be here, would I?"

After the interview, interest in the story finally started to wane, but only a little. It still flared up whenever one of his movies came out and when newspaper circulation started to drop. Occasionally, there were a few unverified speculations about the couple's possible divorce, but the two of them stayed together, far happier than any two lucky people had any right to be.

* * *

Maurice was annoyed when he found out that all of their worry had been for nothing. It turned out that the "Big Plan" for the night always included Declan's spirit being reunited with his mother in Happyland and Cal taking over the Irish hunk's now-vacant body.

"Why didn't they just tell us that in the first place?" he complained to Leonard over drinks when their shift had ended.

"I dunno." Leonard shrugged as he finished his cocktail. "Mysterious ways and all that, I guess."

"Seems like an extra stupid way to get things done."

"Sure, but do you want to tell them that?"

"No."

"I didn't think so."

The Hunt

As he drove over to the restaurant, the only thing Bruce could think about was his palms. They were sweaty. Insanely sweaty. A virtual monsoon of clammy perspiration seeped out of them at a rate that he had never before considered. He actually had to stop the car and grab a towel from his gym bag in the trunk so he could wipe them off. He didn't want Mr. Greystone to know just how nervous he really was.

When he finally drove into the restaurant's parking lot, he grabbed the towel one last time and gave his palms a final wipe down. He then took a deep breath, got out of the car and walked into the restaurant. Dino and Davy's was a quiet Italian steak joint that was popular with older businessmen and guys who wished they were Frank Sinatra. Mr. Greystone was already there, sitting at his usual corner table. Bruce took another deep breath and headed toward him.

"Hello, Mr. Greystone," he said with his hand outstretched.

Mr. Greystone looked up from the menu he was studying and smiled. "Bruce, good to see you." He grabbed Bruce's hand and shook it. After a few seconds Bruce attempted to let go of the shake, but Mr. Greystone held onto his hand. "Nervous, are we?" the older man asked. Bruce gulped and nodded. Mr. Greystone laughed and released his grip on the young man's hand. "Sit down, sit down," he ordered Bruce pleasantly. Bruce quickly complied. "And I've told you before, you can call me Tony," Mr. Greystone reminded him as he lifted his hand to catch the waiter's attention. "There's no need for you to be so formal." Bruce nodded, even though the thought of calling Mr. Greystone by his first name terrified him.

Spurred by Mr. Greystone's signal, a waiter appeared at their table and poured Bruce a glass of water.

"Are you gentlemen ready to order?" he asked.

"Not just yet," answered Mr. Greystone, "but I think we could start off with a few beverages. I'll have a martini."

"Very good, sir. And what can I get you?" he asked Bruce.

"Aum, water's fine with me," Bruce insisted.

"He'll have a martini too," Mr. Greystone told the waiter.

"Very good, sir," the waiter nodded and disappeared toward the bar.

"I don't usually drink," Bruce explained to the older man.

"Don't worry," Mr. Greystone said, laughing, "a little gin and vermouth isn't going to kill you. Plus it'll help take care of whatever's making you so damn jittery."

Bruce smiled weakly, but the truth was that he had two very good reasons to be nervous that night. The first was that Mr. Greystone was his boss, and the second was that he was about to ask the man's permission to marry his only daughter. He knew that Mr. Greystone only loved two things: his business and Suzie, and he knew what the man was capable of doing if anyone hurt either of them. He had heard the story about the salesman who once called Suzie a highly offensive name when she refused to accept his invitation for a drink. The guy was found in a dumpster in another state three days later. He was alive, but just barely. Then there was the story of Peterson, who missed an important meeting with a client because his wife went into labor. When the client then decided to go with another company, Mr. Greystone fired Peterson, had the bank repossess his house and car and sent his wife pictures taken during the last office Christmas party. She divorced him and got sole custody of their baby daughter. Mr. Greystone played extremely rough and Bruce (who had inherited Peterson's job at the company) knew that what he was about to do would put him in a very precarious position, one that most sane men would never put themselves in against their will, much less voluntarily. But the thing was, those sane men had never met Suzie. Bruce had and he knew she was worth the risk.

Suzie was perfect—so perfect that her little insignificant imperfections only highlighted just how perfect the rest of her was. She was smart, friendly, witty and kind. She could kick butt at chess, but preferred to play Twister. She had a smile that not only made other people feel good when they saw it, it made them feel special, as if they had seen one of those comets that only passes by the earth every thousand years or so. She could quote both Shakespeare and the Marx Brothers. Despite her supermodel figure, she loved food and ate like a horse. She adored animals and seemed to have an almost psychic connection with dogs. Truthfully, her only real flaw was that she loved him, despite his countless imperfections, when she could have had anyone she wanted. Knowing all of this, Bruce had decided that he had to marry her as soon as humanly possible—which led him to this terrifying moment in the restaurant with her father.

He reached for a menu, but Mr. Greystone shook his head. "Have the New York steak," he insisted. "It's the only reason to come to this place." Bruce nodded and the waiter returned with their martinis. Mr. Greystone took a sip from his and smiled. Bruce followed suit and tried his damnedest not to wince, which was hard because he was certain he had just swallowed gasoline.

"Are you ready to order?" asked the waiter.

"Yes. We'll have two New Yorks. Hold the salads."

"And how would you like your steaks cooked?"

"Rare," answered Mr. Greystone. "As rare as you can legally serve it."

The waiter nodded and turned to go, but he stopped when Bruce—almost against his own will and definitely against his better judgment—spoke up. "Actually, could I get mine well-done?"

"Certainly, sir," the waiter responded before he left their table.

Bruce felt Mr. Greystone's eyes burn into him. That hadn't been a good move.

"I'm not good with undercooked meat," he explained. "It makes me gag."

Mr. Greystone stared at him for a very long moment before he burst into a loud gale of laughter. "You must really want to marry my Suzie if you're willing to let me push you around like that," he howled as he slapped the table, nearly spilling their martinis.

Bruce was taken aback. "You mean you know?"

"Of course," Mr. Greystone replied, "why else would you ask to have dinner with me? The two of you have been dating for six months now. I'm just surprised it took you this long. Suzie being perfect and all."

"So it's okay with you? I have your permission?" he asked eagerly.

"I didn't say that," Mr. Greystone answered with a grin.

"Pardon me?"

"You're a good kid, Bruce, but I'm not sure you have what it takes to be a part of this family."

"What do you mean?"

"I mean I need Suzie to marry someone with a real killer instinct. Someone who can take over the business I've worked so hard to build over these past 30 years. I'm sure you love her very much and would make a great husband, but I can't have my daughter marrying a wuss. I'm sure you understand."

"But... But..." Bruce was too stunned to even protest.

"If I were you I'd forget about Suzie and think about asking out that cute junior executive I just hired. I think her name is Joyce...or Jill...something with a J. I know company policy frowns on our employees dating, but in this case I'm willing to make an exception."

"But... But..." Bruce tried again to little effect.

"And don't worry about Suzie. A girl like her should have no problem finding someone else."

Snap!

That was the sound that Bruce's brain made when he went from stunned confusion to blind rage. In that moment he forgot where he was and who he was sitting with. All he knew was that his Suzie was being taken away from him and he could not let it happen.

"No!" he shouted and stood up, causing the table to fall over with a tremendous crash. "That's not going to happen! I don't care if we don't have your permission and I don't care if you fire me! All I care about is marrying your daughter, whether you like it or not!" He stared down at Mr. Greystone, not knowing what would happen next.

"Well, that's more like it!" said the older man, grinning. "There's a fire in that belly of yours after all. It's good to see!"

"What—" Bruce immediately switched back from anger to confusion. "Does this mean I have your permission?" he asked, more than a bit bewildered.

"Not yet, but you're getting closer."

Bruce flopped back down into his chair as a group of waiters arrived to prop the table back up and clean up the mess he made.

"I'll have another martini," Mr. Greystone told one of them as they lifted up the table.

"Me too," sighed Bruce.

They sat in silence for a moment, until the waiters were finished and they were alone again.

"What do I have to do?" asked Bruce. "How can I prove to you that I'm worthy of marrying Suzie?"

Mr. Greystone's face broke into a lupine grin. "Have you ever gone hunting?" he asked.

Bruce shook his head. He had never so much as gone fishing or camping, much less hunting.

"You can learn a lot about a person by taking them hunting," Mr. Greystone explained. "But most importantly, you can learn if they have the killer instinct a person needs to be a good businessman."

"You want me to go hunting with you?"

"Yes."

"Is that all?"

"Trust me," Mr. Greystone said with a laugh, "it'll be enough."

At that moment two waiters appeared with their steaks and fresh martinis. Mr. Greystone dug into his with an almost feral glee, but not before looking disdainfully at Bruce's well-done entree.

"What a waste of a good piece of beef," he grumbled before he stuffed a huge chunk of dripping red meat into his mouth.

* * *

When Bruce got back home he noticed that Suzie's car was parked in front of his apartment. He found her sitting in front of his TV watching one of those reality shows where a group of strangers gets stranded together and tortured by the show's producers.

"How'd it go?"

"I don't know," he admitted. "I have to go hunting with him."

"Are you serious?"

"Yeah. He says he's not sure that I have the right killer instinct he thinks a husband of yours needs."

"You do know he's insane, right?"

"Of course, but he's your dad. What else can I do?"

"Tell him where to stick it," she answered him without a trace of sarcasm.

"I can't do that. He may be your dad, but he's also my boss. Anyway, I already tried. Sorta. He just laughed and told me I had to go hunting with him."

"What else did he say?"

"He told me that if I ever ordered a well-done steak in his presence again, he wouldn't be responsible for his actions. That was about it."

"He didn't say anything about the hunt?"

"We're going on Friday, after work. We're supposed to be back Sunday night, but I got the impression that he doesn't think I'm man enough to last the whole weekend."

Suzie reached over to him from the couch and he sat down beside her and gave her a warm hug.

"Don't go," she whispered.

"What?"

"Don't go hunting with my father."

"Please, Suzie," Bruce pleaded, "don't put me in this position. You know I can't afford to alienate him."

"I know, but I still don't want you to go. And it's not like this is the 1800s and you need my father's blessing to marry me. I'm a big girl and I can take care of myself."

"Tell that to the guy they found in the dumpster."

"What?"

"Never mind," Bruce sighed. "I have to go," he insisted. "If I don't, he'll never respect me again, which would be fine if he was just my father-in-law, but he's also my boss and if I'm going to get anywhere in his company, I can't have him thinking I'm a big wussy girliepants."

"But you *are* a big wussy girliepants," she teased.

"Yeah, but he doesn't have to know that."

"This isn't about your manhood being questioned, is it? Because that is so lame if it is."

"It has nothing to do with that," Bruce lied. "And what's the big deal anyway? It's not like you have a problem with people killing animals. Not with the amount of meat you eat or the number of leather shoes you own."

"Just don't go. Please." She armed her request with that adorable pouty-faced look she used whenever she really wanted him to do something against his better judgment.

"You're killing me," he sighed. "How about this? I'll go out with him, but I swear I won't shoot anything."

"I wasn't worried about that," she snorted with laughter.

"What's that supposed to mean?"

"It means the chances of you actually killing anything are zero to none. That's not why I don't want you to go."

"Then what is it?"

"I don't want you to be out alone in the woods with my dad. He gets funny out there."

"Define funny."

"Trust me," she insisted.

"How about this," he attempted one last time. "I'll tell him that I have to meet him at the cabin, instead of driving out there with him. That way if he does start acting peculiar, I can hop in my car and drive back home right away. Would that make you feel better about this?"

"All right, but don't say I didn't warn you."

"Consider me warned, El Capitane," he thanked her with a mock salute.

* * *

Bruce was just about to get into his car to leave for the cabin when his cell phone began to ring.

"Hello?"

"You really don't have to go," Suzie said.

"Yes I do," he insisted. "We already went over this."

"Fine, but remember what you promised. The very first second my dad starts acting weird, you have to hop in your car and drive home. You got that?"

"Loud and clear."

"And don't think you can just humor me," she continued. "If anything happens I will find out about it, and if you think my dad is someone you don't want to mess with, wait 'til you see what I'm capable of," she informed him.

"I like it when you act all tough," he teased. "It's very sexy."

He could tell by her pause that this had made her laugh, but she didn't want him to hear it.

"Just remember what you promised," she said a few seconds later, her voice wavering slightly from its steely demeanor.

"I'll remember," he assured her.

* * *

It took Bruce two hours longer to get to the cabin than he had planned. He got lost twice and it was only by chance that he managed to turn down the right road when he did. When he got there, he found Mr. Greystone sitting on the cabin's porch dressed in a plaid shirt and khakis and smoking a pipe.

"You really go all out," Bruce risked teasing him.

Mr. Greystone smiled. "Have trouble finding the place?" he asked instead.

"Yeah," Bruce admitted. "I got lost."

"Good," said Mr. Greystone. "I didn't want this to be a place any fool could stumble upon. You really have to look for it, don't you?"

"Yes, sir," Bruce agreed.

Mr. Greystone's smile vanished instantly and was replaced by a stern frown. "That," he ordered Bruce, "is the last time you are to call me 'sir' this weekend. You got that?"

"Yes, s—" Bruce had to catch himself. "Sure thing, Tony," he tried again.

"Okay, now that we've got that settled, it's time to eat!" He stood up and walked into the cabin.

"So far, so good," Bruce whispered under his breath as he followed him inside.

The cabin smelled of roasting meat, but it was a kind of meat that Bruce had never smelled before.

"What is that? Venison?" he guessed, assuming that in this setting Mr. Greystone would eat nothing but game.

Mr. Greystone just smiled and shook his head as he opened up the oven of the cabin's wood stove and pulled out a black roasting pan. He rested the pan on the small kitchen counter and lifted up its lid, causing the meat's aroma to increase a hundred-fold throughout the small space. It smelled amazing.

"Makes your mouth water, doesn't it?" Mr. Greystone asked Bruce with a grin.

"Definitely," Bruce answered truthfully as he sat down at the table. "What are we having with it?"

Mr. Greystone laughed. "We're in the wild, Bruce. We don't have to pretend here like we do in the civilized world. You and I both know eating is all about the meat and that all of that other side stuff is for wimps, wusses and women. I don't believe in vegetables. Not out here." A look of challenge filled his eyes. "You don't have a problem with that, do you?"

Bruce could tell that he was being tested, so even though he personally preferred a nice salad to a large hunk of meat, he shook his head. "Not at all," he answered.

"Good."

With that, Mr. Greystone grabbed a very large knife from a drawer and cut up the roast. He divided the pieces in half, put them onto two plates and placed one in front of Bruce. Bruce looked down at it. The meat smelled terrific, but there was so much of it—at least four times what he would normally eat in one sitting—and he could tell that Mr. Greystone expected him to eat it all. The meat was still very rare and he hadn't lied when he had told Mr. Greystone in the restaurant that under-cooked meat made him gag. Plus, he still didn't know what kind of meat it was. As these thoughts swirled in his head, he closed his eyes and thought of Suzie. That was enough to make him to pick up his knife and fork and start eating.

He had to fight his instinct to gag, but he managed to swallow his first bite. The flavor was completely new to him. It was good, even better than it smelled. He took another bite and then another. By his fifth mouthful, he didn't even mind that it wasn't well done.

"This is delicious."

"I know," the older man grinned almost conspiratorially.

That was it for dinner conversation, and the two men continued to stuff their faces with the extremely tasty red meat. It took Bruce a full half-hour to finish his plate, but he did finish it. Mr. Greystone watched with an amused expression as the young man wolfed down the exotic-tasting meat.

"That is what the hunt is all about," he explained to Bruce when they were both done. "You can't get anything like that at the supermarket or at a restaurant. You have to go out and get it yourself. People think hunting is all about men getting in touch with their primal selves—and I suppose it is—but it's also about the flavor. Have you ever tasted anything like that before?"

"No, I haven't." Bruce had to whisper. He was so full he could barely talk.

"Unfortunately, that was all I had left in my freezer. That's why I wanted to come out here this weekend. It's time for me to restock."

"I don't know how much help I'll be," Bruce admitted. "I've never gone hunting before."

"You'll do just fine."

"So I suppose you want to go out first thing tomorrow, huh? This is a crack of dawn sort of deal, right?"

"Actually, I prefer to do my hunting at night."

"Really?"

"Yes. It makes it much more exciting."

Bruce couldn't help but wonder if this was the kind of thing Suzie had warned him about. But then again he knew virtually nothing about hunting, so he had no idea if going out at night was crazy or not.

"Do you want to go out right now?" he asked.

"In a few minutes," Mr. Greystone said. "I'll give you some time to digest your meal."

* * *

Bruce's cell phone rang. Normally he would have answered it, but he had forgotten to take it with him into the cabin. After the fifth ring it switched over to his voice mail and Suzie left her third message of the night.

"Why aren't you answering your stupid phone, you pinhead?" She cursed at him impatiently. "Call me back right away and remember your promise!" she ordered before she hung up.

In the cabin, Mr. Greystone was ready to go. Bruce was still feeling drowsy from all the meat he had eaten, but he still managed to get up and get dressed in the closest thing he had to hunting attire: a pair of jeans and white sneakers, a wool sweater and a nylon pullover. His outfit elicited a frown from Mr. Greystone, but the older man didn't say anything. Bruce followed him outside.

"Aren't we forgetting something?"

"What?" Mr. Greystone replied.

"Don't we need some kind of weapon? Like a shotgun or something?"

Mr. Greystone nodded and pulled a large handgun from out of his plaid jacket. He handed it to Bruce, who didn't expect it to be so heavy and almost dropped it as a result.

"People hunt with handguns?" he asked dubiously.

"Not normally," said Mr. Greystone, "but this isn't what anyone would call a normal hunt."

Bruce nodded slowly while he reached into his pullover pocket to make sure his car keys were still there. They weren't.

"Looking for these?" Mr. Greystone held the keys up and jangled them playfully.

"How did—" Bruce started before Mr. Greystone interrupted him.

"A trick I learned in my youth," he explained. "I'm sorry to have to resort to petty thievery in order to keep you here, but I'm sure that Suzie ordered you to bolt the moment things got weird, and I can't have that, can I? Not with an empty freezer, that's for sure."

"What's going on?" Bruce was doing his damnedest not to panic, but his damnedest wasn't good enough. His whole body started to nervously shake.

"Oh come on," Mr. Greystone said. "Haven't you figured it all out by now?"

Bruce shook his head. He didn't have a clue.

Mr. Greystone frowned.

"I bet you were one of those kids who covered your eyes during the scary parts when you went to the movies, weren't you?" he guessed accusingly.

"No," Bruce protested lamely. As a kid he refused to see any movie that had scary parts in it, so covering his eyes never actually came up.

"Well, you're obviously not a fan of horror movies or else you'd recognize what is obviously a fairly standard situation."

"Are you going to kill me?" Bruce gulped with terror, forgetting that he was the one holding the gun.

"Maybe," Mr. Greystone admitted. "The night has just begun and the hunt hasn't even started yet, but the plan is for you to be dead when the sun rises."

"You're going to hunt me?"

"Of course not." Mr. Greystone shook his head. "That wouldn't be fair. We're going to hunt each other."

"You're crazy!"

"Sure I am," Mr. Greystone said, "but who isn't these days?"

"But why?"

"It's simple. You need to prove to me that you're man enough to marry my daughter and I need to restock my freezer. That's all there is to it."

"What do you mean, 'restock'? Was that—what we ate—was that—"

"That was Peterson," Mr. Greystone said calmly.

"Peterson?" Bruce refused to believe his ears.

Mr. Greystone rolled his eyes impatiently. "Yes, Peterson. The guy you replaced. You just ate him and you thought he was delicious."

Bruce thought for a second before he bent over and threw up. Three times. Mr. Greystone waited quietly as the tender young man did his best to rid his body of the meal he had just enjoyed.

Dizzy and exhausted, Bruce was still bent over when he finally spoke. "You're a monster," he said. His voice was hoarse and his words were slightly slurred.

"Yes," Mr. Greystone agreed.

"A cannibal."

"Oh, no," Mr. Greystone disagreed. "I'm not a cannibal."

Bruce managed to stand up and finally realized he still had a gun in his hand. "How can you say that? You eat people!" He pointed the weapon at his almost father-in-law.

"Yes," Mr. Greystone agreed, showing not the slightest bit of concern over the raised gun aimed in his direction. "But in order to be a cannibal I would have to be a person myself. It's a technicality, I know, but it still applies."

"What are you talking about?" Bruce shouted as the gun shook in his hand.

"It's simple," explained Mr. Greystone, "I agreed with you when you called me a monster, and that's because I am a monster."

"What?"

Mr. Greystone sighed.

"Even a little mincing pantywaist like yourself has to have seen a few movies with monsters in them, right? And if you have, then you should know that in the monster world there are the three main contenders. You got your vampires, your Frankenstein zombie types and your werewolves. I'll give you one guess which one I am and I'll even give you a couple of hints. I have a great tan and I can speak in full sentences. Can you figure it out?"

Bruce stopped shaking and put down the gun. Mr. Greystone was obviously toying with him, but now he had taken it too far. Monsters? Even he wasn't naive enough to fall for that.

"This is the test, right?" He smiled uneasily. "I'm supposed to get all weak-kneed and turn tail and run into the forest just because you tell me that you're some kind of monster? What do I look like? The world's biggest idiot? I can't believe I fell for that bit about eating Peterson. What did we really eat? Goat? Moose? And this gun," Bruce smirked, "I bet it isn't even loaded." To prove it, he pulled the trigger. The loudest sound he ever heard exploded from his hand as a bullet fired out of the gun's muzzle and hit the ground, just an inch away from his right foot. He screamed and dropped the gun, much to Mr. Greystone's amusement.

"This is going to be too easy."

"Why was that loaded?" Bruce demanded, in a high-pitched voice "You're taking it too far!"

"I told you, Bruce," Mr. Greystone reminded him, "it hasn't even started. And you haven't guessed yet."

"About what?" Bruce shook, still frightened from the gunshot.

"The kind of monster I am!" Mr. Greystone shouted.

"I don't know!" Bruce shouted back.

"I gave you hints! I told you I have a nice tan, which means I can't be a vampire, and I can speak in complete sentences, which means I'm not a mindless zombie, so that means I have to be a...."

"Werewolf?" Bruce answered meekly.

"Give the boy a prize!" Mr. Greystone yelled triumphantly.

"But that's impossible," Bruce insisted. "Werewolves don't exist and even if they did they only transform during full moons."

Mr. Greystone shook his head. "Sorry, Bruce, but even Hollywood can't get everything right."

"What are you talking about?"

"What I'm saying is that all of that stuff about werewolves needing a full moon to transform is bunk. We can change whenever we feel like it—morning, noon or night, 24 hours a day, seven days a week, even on Christmas."

"I don't believe you!"

Mr. Greystone rolled his eyes and started unbuttoning his jacket. He took it off and then started unbuttoning his shirt.

"What are you doing?" Bruce asked.

"Proving a point, so we can get started." Mr. Greystone removed his shirt, revealing a torso far more muscular than you would expect from a man of his years. He lifted up his arms and stretched them out as if he was warming up for the beginning of a workout. He did this for a minute before he stopped and became still. He then closed his eyes and tensed every muscle in his body. Bruce watched as beads of sweat began to pour out of the man's skin. Even standing 10 feet away he could hear the sound of something rumbling inside Mr. Greystone's body. Before his eyes, thick gray hair began to grow all over the man. Mr. Greystone's face began to contort and change. His nose started protruding from his face, forming—with his mouth—into a long snout. His muscles grew larger and harder, and long claws grew out from his fingers, which grew shorter and less human. Sharp teeth protruded from his snout, as he began to growl. The transformation appeared to be complete; before Bruce stood a terrifying combination of man and beast capable of walking erect while possessing the feral animal ferocity of a 400-pound hellhound.

Bruce screamed and ran. He didn't make it two feet before he tripped over the gun he had dropped and fell to the ground with a painful thud. He turned on his back and froze with terror as the monster in front of him howled with delight before transforming back into the form of his almost father-in-law.

"Do you believe me now?" Mr. Greystone smiled.

Bruce answered him by screaming once again.

"Oh, be quiet," Mr. Greystone shushed him, "or else you aren't going to hear the rules."

Bruce stopped screaming, but his heart beat so loudly he could still barely hear what Mr. Greystone was saying.

"They are very simple. If you make it to Sunday morning's sunrise without me clawing open one of your major

arteries, then you get to marry Suzie. If you don't, then marriage really won't be an option. So the odds aren't completely stacked against you. You'll be able to use the gun to defend yourself, but you'll find the bullets I've provided won't do you much good. That's why, to make it interesting, I've hidden a clip full of silver bullets in the surrounding woods. Find it and you just may have a chance." He then walked over to cabin's porch and grabbed a blue duffel bag that had been lying under it. He dropped the bag beside Bruce, who still cowered on the ground.

"In here you'll find other supplies that will hopefully help this hunt last longer than five minutes. Also, I'm going to be super generous and give you an hour head start. Again, I'm afraid it won't do you much good, because I'll be able to smell your scent from at least 40 miles away."

He then walked over to Bruce's car. "And to make sure you don't try and escape by doing something silly like driving away…"

He lifted up its hood and grabbed hold of a part that looked important and ripped it out as if it were a petal on a flower.

"Okay, that's it. You've got an hour. If I were you I'd be running like hell right now."

Bruce didn't have to be told twice. He picked up the gun and the bag, which was very heavy, and jumped to his feet and ran the woods as fast as his legs could carry him.

Inside Bruce's car his cell phone rang. Suzie left another message on his voice mail.

"Bruce, I'm serious," she pleaded, "where are you? I'm getting all these visions of my dad doing something truly nuts. I swear, if you don't call me back within the next half hour, I'm going to drive over there and take you home myself."

* * *

Bruce had run far longer and far faster than ever before. Were it not for the combination of fear and adrenaline coursing through his veins, he would have collapsed 10 minutes ago. But even fear and adrenaline could only do so much. Now his legs simply could not allow him to move any further. Exhausted, he collapsed to the ground, falling on something hard, prickly and quite possibly, poisonous. He dropped the gun in his hand and the blue duffel bag crashed loudly as it collided with the forest's floor. He had been running for a half-hour, which meant he had another 30 minutes before the monster started stalking him. He tried in vain to catch his breath, but his heart raced like never before. He wondered if it would burst right there in his chest, unable to handle the strain. His whole body was covered in a layer of sticky, viscous sweat that stuck to his clothes and smelled so bad. A *person* could have smelled him from 40 miles away, let alone an inhuman monster salivating at the thought of a well-stocked freezer.

Knowing that every second he spent not moving was a second closer to his demise, he forced himself to sit up. His legs refused to move, so he busied himself by searching through the duffel bag to see what was inside. He had to do it mostly by feel, as the quarter moon above him was his only light and even its fluorescence was dimmed by the trees overhead. The first item felt like a pair of binoculars, its lenses covered. By accident his hand brushed against a switch near his temple and he pressed it in hopes that something would happen. Two green lights turned on inside the glasses and at once he could see the forest around him.

Night vision goggles, he thought, remembering a TV show he had seen in which a group of soldiers had used glasses like this during a late-night raid. *Well, one problem solved.* Using the goggles, he looked into the bag and found a canteen filled with fresh water. Without thinking he uncapped it and drank it dry. His body was satisfied, but he cursed himself for not saving any water for the hours ahead. He went back to the bag and found a very sharp Bowie knife, a small first-aid kit, a length of rope, a piece of chalk, some beef jerky (at least, he hoped it was beef jerky) and a small map that apparently led to the silver bullets.

The map was useless to Bruce, since he had no clue where he was in relation to it. Even with the ability to see at night, all he saw were trees, none of which were distinctive enough to offer any clues about his location. He worried that he would just end up moving toward Mr. Greystone rather than away from him. He considered marking trees with the piece of chalk as he traveled, but then he realized that that would just lead his monstrous employer directly to him.

He put everything back into the duffel bag except for the goggles, which he kept on. He tried to stand up. At first his legs refused, as they still ached beyond all reason, but eventually he rose unsteadily to his feet. He had 15 minutes left before Mr. Greystone would begin chasing him. He looked around and realized he couldn't remember which direction he had been running.

"The moon was in front of me," he reminded himself without much conviction. Hoping his memory was right, he decided to keep moving toward the moon.

He limped forward as fast as he could. His legs hurt so much.

* * *

Mr. Greystone waited impatiently for the hour to pass. He briefly considered cheating and beginning his pursuit of Bruce before the hour had ended, but he was an infernal supernatural creature of the darkness who kept his word, so he stayed put. The truth was he almost felt sorry for the poor guy, who really had no chance at all. He wouldn't be surprised if he found Bruce after 10 minutes in the forest, having fallen and broken a leg or accidentally impaled himself on a sharp tree branch. He wondered what Suzie could possibly see in him. He knew it wasn't the guy's looks, charm or wealth, because even a generous observer would deem Bruce homely, nervous and poor. What was it then that endeared the sweaty little man to someone as perfect as Suzie?

"She's probably just sticking it to her old man," he answered aloud as he used a toothpick to unwedge a tiny morsel of Peterson from between two of his back molars.

He sighed as the minutes ticked slowly on his watch. He enjoyed the thrill of the contest almost as much as he loved the flavor of the meat, and a part of him hoped that he was wrong and that somehow—against all odds—Bruce would prove to be a worthy adversary.

He inhaled deeply through his nose. He wasn't in wolf form so he could only barely detect Bruce's scent in the forest, but he could smell the subtle shift in the air. The weather was about to change.

It was going to rain.

* * *

Wearing the goggles made running through the forest much easier than it had been before. Bruce could now see everything in his path and was able to avoid doing something stupid like breaking his leg or getting impaled on a sharp tree branch. He could even see animals scurry away from him in the distance, all of them wary of his approach. As he ran he became more and more concerned about the malodorous sweat that covered his body. He knew that if he didn't do something to get rid of it, it would take Mr. Greystone only a few minutes to find him.

Just as he began to despair about what he was going to do, he caught his first real break of the hunt. Rain began to fall. The droplets were heavy, hard and fast. Normally he would have cursed his misfortune, but at that moment, getting drenched was the greatest thing that had ever happened to him. He quickly stripped out of his clothes and washed himself in the heavy rain. As cold and wet as he was, all he felt was elation as the thick layer of sweat was cleansed from his body.

Or was it? Bruce wondered just how powerful Mr. Greystone's sense of smell was when he was a wolf. Perhaps even a rain like this wasn't enough to get rid Bruce of his telltale odor. Out of time and with the hunt officially started two minutes ago, he took a second to think of what more he could do. His eyes fell to the ground and watched as the water collected in large puddles and turned the ground to mud.

Mud.

Once it occurred to him, he didn't hesitate. He fell to his knees and rolled on the ground. He grabbed large handfuls of mud and smeared it across his naked body until he was completely covered. He then threw his clothes into the duffel bag, put his goggles back on and started running once more.

At that moment he knew that somewhere, something greater than himself was on his side, because as he ran the rain stopped, almost as if it had fallen to give him this chance for survival.

* * *

Mr. Greystone wasn't worried about the rain. He knew what Bruce could do with it if he had the slightest bit of sense, but he was certain that the guy was so panic-stricken he would think of nothing except running as fast as he could. He looked down at his watch and smiled when it was time to begin.

The smile remained as he removed his shirt and jacket and took off his watch, just like he had for his previous transformation. This time, he also removed his pants, not wanting them to tear as he ran through the woods. He stretched his arms and legs for a minute, and then tensed his body and made the switch. It literally did feel like flipping a switch in his mind. All he had to do was concentrate and it would flip from man to animal and vice versa. But, unlike what most would assume, the switch only affected his physical being. It did nothing to his mind, which was always partly human and partly wolf. He was exactly the same person no matter what he looked like on the outside. He just played the part of man when he had to deal with other people in the real world, and he became the wolf when he needed to hunt or take care of the seedier sides of his company's affairs.

The transformation hurt, but the pain lasted only as long as the process took to complete. When it was over, he felt nothing but the power of his heightened senses. As the wolf, he was faster and stronger than any man who ever lived. He could see at night and hear sounds from miles away, but he depended the most on his sense of smell to find his prey.

Bruce's odor was so heavy it almost hurt to breathe it in. Salivating at the thought of the meal he would have next morning, he howled joyfully and followed the scent as fast as his body would propel him.

* * *

Bruce almost threw up when he heard the wolf's howl echo through the forest. He was now being pursued and he had no idea how far he had run or where he was. He didn't know if his muddy camouflage would do him any good or if it would just get him captured quicker. He took a little comfort in knowing that the howl had come from a long way behind him, so he had been running in the right direction.

Both the gun, which he held in his right hand, and the duffel bag that he had strapped to his back, felt far heavier now than when he began. He was going to have to lose some items. He knew he would end up regretting the loss of whatever he threw away, but at that moment, he had no other option. He stopped and opened the bag and threw away the rope, the canteen, the chalk and the first-aid kit. He grabbed the Bowie knife, which sat in a leather scabbard, and strapped it to his left thigh. All that was left inside the bag were his clothes, the map to the silver bullets and the package of beef jerky. They were light enough to keep, but as he looked at them he thought of a very good reason to throw all but the map away. He took the small piece of paper and stuffed it into the scabbard, and took out the knife and started cutting his clothes into strips. He then ran to a tree and tied a strip of his shirt on one of its branches. He grabbed a piece of jerky and wrapped a strip of his pants around it and dropped it on the ground. He threw the rest of the strips into the duffel bag and started running again.

He hoped it would work.

* * *

Suzie was torn between being really mad and really worried as she drove toward her dad's cabin. She hoped she could find it, as she had only been there once before and that was years ago. She had hated it there. She was a city girl and the wilderness—as far as she was concerned—was just a place to go if you were really into bug bites or mysterious red rashes.

As she drove she tried calling Bruce again and swore loudly when she got his voice mail for the seventh time. She cursed him for not answering his phone, but then felt guilty, knowing that the reason for his silence was likely because he was out doing something insane with her dad.

She and her father had never really gotten along. He loved her more than anything, but he loved her like a piece of property and not a living, breathing person who might have thoughts and attitudes different from his. That's why she loved Bruce. He was the first person she had ever met who made her feel loved for just being around and not for what her good looks and intelligence did to prop up his own personal social cachet. That was why she wanted to marry him and why it was so important that nothing happen to him while he was out alone in the wild with her insane dad.

* * *

The scent of Bruce's terror was so heavy in the forest that Mr. Greystone almost choked on it. It surrounded him like something he could reach out and grab. If the shape of his snout had allowed him a chortle, he would have laughed aloud. He drooled instead, his teeth glistening at the thought of what the fool's flesh would taste like. He knew it would be better than Peterson's because Bruce was younger and flabbier—making for a more tender and flavorful meat. He howled in anticipation, thrilled to think that Bruce would hear this cry in the dark and know his doom was only a moment or two away.

* * *

Bruce did hear the howl, but instead of filling him with terror, it only confirmed that his plan might actually be working. For the past half-hour he had abandoned all attempts at following a straightforward path, and instead ran chaotically through the forest, tying bits of his clothing to trees. When he finally ran out of clothes, he turned around and began running in the direction of the wolf's howls, hoping it would lead him back to the cabin. There he would find his cell phone, call for help and steal Mr. Greystone's car, which the older man hadn't been wise enough to sabotage. His boss wasn't the only one who had experimented with delinquency in his teens; Bruce had hotwired a car or two in his past.

"I can do this," he whispered to himself as he ran through the woods, his body now so used to the pain he no longer felt it. "I can actually do this."

* * *

It felt like running into a brick wall. Almost at once, the scent that had been so strong virtually disappeared.

The rain! Mr. Greystone remembered. *The little fool was smart enough to take advantage of the rain!*

He stopped and decided to wait for a few minutes. Bruce wasn't smart enough to get rid of the smell completely, so a trace of it still had to be out there. It was just a matter of finding it, which would take a little time, since the scent was still so abundant in his nostrils; he would have to separate the real thing from his recollection of it.

As he worked to recapture the scent, he felt a mixture of annoyance and pleasure. He was annoyed to find he would actually have to work for his supper, but he was thrilled to discover that Bruce might prove to be a worthy adversary after all.

I underestimated that boy, he thought as he caught a whiff of Bruce's scent in the distance. It was weak and nowhere near as certain as it had been before, but it was enough for Mr. Greystone to go on. He turned to follow it.

Now the hunt was truly on.

* * *

Suzie was lost. She suspected her dad chose a cabin that was deliberately hard to find. She drove for another half-hour before she found the turn she had missed and finally reached her father's cabin.

She didn't like what she found there. The hood to Bruce's car was up and its engine had been damaged. She looked through the driver's side window and saw his cell phone sitting in one of the cup holders. Bruce had no idea she was out here.

The cabin was empty. She could tell they had eaten in there because of the dirty plates on the table and the counter, and the lingering aroma of roasted Peterson in the air.

"I'm too late," she said out loud. Whatever the two of them were doing, they were out there doing it. Having no other choice, she sighed, sat down on the cabin's dingy sofa and waited for them to come back.

* * *

The scent grew stronger as Mr. Greystone approached. Bruce must have stopped moving, either because of exhaustion or some kind of incapacitating accident. Whatever the case, he was now going to be easy prey.

Sensing Bruce was only half a mile away, he ran as fast as he could, with his teeth bared and his claws outstretched. He ran and ran, but when he reached the spot where the scent was coming from, he found nothing. Nothing except a piece of torn material tied around a tree branch. Mr. Greystone howled angrily at this discovery, but he stopped when he caught the scent again. This time it was moving.

You think you're so clever, he mocked Bruce before chasing after the newly caught scent. It was only a short distance away and took him two minutes to find it. It wasn't Bruce. It was a skunk carrying a piece of beef jerky in its mouth. Around the jerky was another torn piece of material. Unfortunately for Mr. Greystone, he found this out only after he had pounced on the poor creature, which then did what all skunks do when confronted in this manner. It emptied its glands all over the ferocious werewolf, causing the hellhound to howl in agony as the foul stench invaded his very powerful nose. The skunk raced away and Mr. Greystone fell to the ground, coughing and sputtering as he made the switch in his mind and transformed back into his human shape. The stink was horrible, but with his human senses it was not quite as painful to bear. He rested on the ground and went from feeling foolish and embarrassed to very, very angry.

Now it wasn't about filling his freezer or proving that Bruce was worthy of marrying Suzie. Now it was personal. This was a humiliation that he could not let stand and Bruce was going to suffer for it.

Suffer a lot.

The problem was that he was now working from a disadvantage. Not only could he not trust any trace of Bruce's scent that he came across, but now the nauseating smell of the skunk's spray made it impossible for him to pick it up anyway. Bruce could be anywhere and he no longer had the advantage of his most powerful sense to find him.

It then occurred to him that the simplest solution to his problem was to return to the cabin and wait for Sunday morning. When it did, Bruce would assume that he had prevailed and would come back to where they had started. He would then slaughter the fool, fill his freezer and get some measure of satisfaction for having to spend the next week bathing in tomato juice.

Deciding that this was the perfect plan, he got up and headed back to the cabin, wishing that he hadn't left all of his clothes there, as the chilly night air nipped away at his exposed body.

* * *

Bruce nearly wept when he finally saw the cabin appear in front of him. He noticed that its lights were on and he was relieved when he saw Suzie's car parked right beside his.

"Suzie!" he shouted running the cabin. She appeared in the doorway. He was so happy to see her that he forgot what he must have looked like. When Suzie caught sight of him running at her, naked, covered head to toe in mud, with night vision goggles on, a gun in his hand and a knife strapped to his thigh, she screamed and shut and locked the door.

"Suzie!" he shouted as he pounded on the door. "Open up! It's me. It's Bruce!"

"Bruce?"

"Suzie!" he shouted again.

Slowly the door opened the teeniest bit and he saw Suzie's skeptical eyes studying him through the slit. He took off the goggles and smiled at her.

"What is going on?" she asked him as she opened the door all the way and let him in. Instead of answering her, he burst into tears and hugged her as hard as he could. She let him have his moment before she decided enough was enough. "Seriously," she said as she wedged herself out of his arms, "what is going on?"

"Suzie," he said, his voice hoarse with emotion, "I have something to tell you. You're going to think I'm insane, but I swear I'm not lying to you. It's going to be almost impossible for you to fathom—"

"My dad's a werewolf," she interrupted him. "Yeah, I know. Why are you naked?"

It took Bruce a second to comprehend what she just said. "What do you mean you know?" he asked her.

"Why do you think I didn't want you to go hunting with him? He's a werewolf! He does crazy junk out here in the woods."

"You knew?" he asked again, stuck on this point.

"He's *my dad*."

"And you didn't tell me?" he asked her.

"Would you have believed me?"

"Yeah," he lied.

She gave him one of those "Don't Be An Idiot" looks of hers.

"Okay, no," he admitted. "But you could have warned me!"

"I told you not to go," she reminded him. "What are you two doing anyway?"

"We're hunting each other," he told her.

"Excuse me?"

"If he catches me, then he's going to eat me. If I last until Sunday morning, then I get to marry you."

Suzie couldn't quite believe her ears. "Are you kidding me? Are you *freakin' kidding me?*"

"No," he answered, a bit embarrassed by how stupid the whole thing sounded.

"I'm going to kill him," she said, shaking her head. "He was going to eat you?"

"Yes, he was" answered a voice from the door. It wasn't Bruce's.

Suzie and Bruce coughed as the smell of skunk filled the cabin. They turned and saw Mr. Greystone, looking more than a little peeved.

"Dad!" Suzie shouted at him. "What do you think you're doing?"

"Proving his manhood," he answered as he took looked at the two of them. *Mud!* He thought to himself. *The little bastard covered himself with mud!*

"Did I tell you that it needed proving?" she asked him.

"If he was going to be a part of this family, he needed to prove he could survive!" he insisted.

"What do you mean 'going to be'?"

"I mean, after what I've been through tonight, there's no way he's getting out of here alive!" he snarled.

"Wanna bet?" she retorted.

Bruce eye's darted back and forth as his fiancé stood toe to toe with her father. "Uh, sweetie," his voice barely above a whisper, "maybe you shouldn't get in your dad's face like that."

"Be quiet," she ordered him. "I can take care of this."

"Listen to the wimp," her father advised her. "You don't want to see me when I'm angry."

She rolled her eyes. "Oh *please.* I've seen you angry, and anyway we both know that *I'm* the one you don't want to piss off."

"Suzie!" Mr. Greystone shouted at her. "Get out of my way!"

"No!" she shouted back.

"Suzie," Bruce interrupted, "you really should—"

"Be quiet!" the two of them shouted.

"That's it," Mr. Greystone decided. "You asked for this."

With that, he tensed his body and began to transform into the wolf, causing Bruce to scream out in terror. Suzie watched nonplussed, and when her father stood before her as a snarling hell beast with a look of insane animal fury in its eyes, she shrugged and pretended to yawn.

"Is that all you got?" she asked, a look of fierce determination in her eyes.

"Are you crazy?" Bruce shouted as he ran behind the couch for cover, but she did not respond.

Her father leapt at her, his claws ready to slice her open. She dodged him easily and turned to Bruce.

"Honey," she said to him as she heaved her father over her shoulder and threw him on the ground, "I guess there is no easy way for you to find this out." She kicked her dad in his stomach. "My dad's not the only werewolf in the family."

Suzie tensed her body and grimaced as it sprouted hair and took a new shape. Bruce responded by screaming louder than he had when her dad had done the exact same thing.

Her dad leapt off of the ground and the two wolf-creatures circled each other with their teeth bared and their claws outstretched. Bruce couldn't handle the tension and jumped down behind the sofa and covered his eyes. *This isn't happening,* he said to himself repeatedly. But despite his attempt to deny the reality that was unfolding loudly in front of him, he couldn't block out the earsplitting howl of pain that echoed through the small cabin.

"Suzie!" he jumped up and shouted.

"What?" She looked at him. Human once again, she was standing over the body of her wounded father.

"I love you," he told her sincerely.

"I know," she said. "Do you want to get out of here now?"

He nodded.

The two of them ran out of the cabin and jumped into her car.

"You do know you're still naked?" she asked as she started the car.

"I'll worry about that later," he told her. "Let's just get the hell out of here."

Suzie nodded and shifted into reverse. Bruce's sudden shout alerted her to the danger approaching from in front of her. Her father—far angrier than she had ever seen him as a man or wolf—jumped from the cabin's porch onto the hood of her car.

She hit the pedal as hard as she could, hoping the speed would knock him off balance, but he held on, raised his clawed hand and smashed it into her windshield. The glass shattered and Suzie hit the brakes. Her dad lunged forward and she shifted back to drive and hit the gas again. The car sped forward and this time the change in momentum toppled her father, but as he fell the claws of his left hand pierced the hood and kept him from hitting the ground. He pulled himself up, raised his right hand and punched the hood as hard as he could. His claws went through it. The car's engine cried out as Mr. Greystone drove his hand into it and tore it apart. The car stopped and Suzie and Bruce both jumped out and started running. Her dad jumped off the hood and howled before chasing after them.

Suzie immediately transformed into her wolf form and grabbed her fiancée just as her dad was ready to pounce. She threw Bruce over her shoulder and carried him into the woods. Despite the extra weight, she was still much faster than her father and managed to lose him just as the sun started to rise.

* * *

"Suzie!" Bruce shouted as he bounced on top of her furry shoulder. "Suzie! Stop! We lost him! Stop!"

She stopped, put him down on the ground and transformed back into the woman he loved. Despite running for miles with a 150-pound man over her shoulder, she didn't even appear winded. Her clothes were torn from the strain of her more muscular werewolf form, but they still managed to cover her up.

"Suzie," Bruce tried to speak calmly, but he was winded, despite having exerted virtually no physical effort during their escape. "I—think—we—have—to—talk," he managed between breaths as he lay on the cold ground.

"About the werewolf thing, huh?" she guessed.

He nodded.

"I was going to tell you," she insisted. "I just figured it was best to wait for a more appropriate time—like our 25th wedding anniversary."

"How did you think you were going to hide it?"

"What do you mean?" she asked. "I *was* hiding it. Did you seriously have a clue that I might be a werewolf before an hour or so ago?"

"Well, no," he admitted.

"This is the first time I've done the wolf thing in three years. The last time was when that jerk salesman called me a tease and I left him in a dumpster in another state. I'm a city girl, and wolfing out doesn't really fit in with that kind of lifestyle. I mean, look," she lifted up her arms and performed a quick pirouette, "it's murder on your clothes."

Bruce didn't laugh.

"Oh, c'mon. Don't be like that. I'm still the exact same girl you fell in love with. I'm still Suzie."

Bruce sat up and looked at her. The sun was rising in the sky over her head and even though the image of her other side was burned into his mind, she was still the most beautiful woman he had ever seen.

"At least now I know that you're not perfect." He smiled as he stood up and gave her a long, hard hug.

Suzie hugged him back and—knowing that Bruce was willing to accept her for what she was—she began to cry. "We really shouldn't be doing this," she said as she rested her head on his shoulder and wiped away a tear. "My dad could find us any moment now."

Bruce remembered something and finally let her go. He pulled the map out of the scabbard that was still tied around his thigh.

"What's this?" Suzie asked as he handed it to her.

"It's a map your dad gave me to even things up between us. It's supposed to lead me to where he stashed some silver bullets. If we find them, we can stop him."

Suzie shook her head. "It's a trap," she said.

"How do you know?"

"Silver bullets are just something the movies invented as a way for the heroes to kill werewolves. In reality they're no more effective against us than real bullets."

"And real bullets?"

"Hurt like the dickens, but they barely slow us down."

"So there's nothing we can do to stop him?"

She shrugged. "Nothing except fight him one on one," Suzie said before her eyes filled with the glow of a brilliant idea. "Or *two* on one."

"What do you mean?" asked Bruce. "I can't fight him. He'd slice me open before I even got my fists up."

Suzie smiled. "Do you trust me?"

"Of course," he answered. "What do you have in mind?"

"There's one thing that the movies do manage to get right," she told him, "and that's what happens when someone is bitten by a werewolf and survives. Do you know what that is?"

"The person becomes a werewolf too," he answered, then clued in. "You're going to turn me into a werewolf?"

She nodded. "It's gonna hurt."

"How much?"

"Remember that time when you caught yourself in your zipper?"

"It's going to hurt that much?" Bruce frowned, recalling the worst pain he had ever experienced.

"No." Suzie shook her head. "A lot more."

Bruce paused. This was rapidly turning into the most bizarre weekend of his short life. He wondered what would happen next.

"All right," he finally said. "Let's get it over with."

Suzie tensed her body and switched back into her werewolf form. Bruce stood still as she lunged toward him and sank her sharp teeth into the meat of his right arm. It hurt — a lot. Bruce felt his consciousness slip away from him and he collapsed onto the ground. Suzie waited as the infection coursed through his wound and began traveling through his veins to his heart and his mind.

It would take a few minutes.

* * *

Something had happened to Mr. Greystone's mind. Whatever it was that had allowed him to keep both halves of his psyche in check was no longer working. The wolf side had taken over and his human side could no longer control the animal's desire to destroy. His chest still bled from the wound his own daughter had inflicted upon him, and his only thought was that it must be avenged. The part of him that loved his daughter and wanted to protect her from all harm was no match for the bloodlust that now consumed him. His nose battled against the stink that covered his body as he attempted to find her scent. He could only find traces of it, which wasn't enough for him to know for certain where she was. He was slower than she was, but he was confident that they would have to stop, and when they did he would find them. No matter how hard they fought, they would not survive the encounter.

* * *

The last time Bruce had felt anything like this, he had been 14 and undergoing his last significant growth spurt. The infection was playing havoc with his insides, rearranging them so they could accommodate the physical change his body would now be able to make at will. His head burned, as if consumed by the kind of fever most people did not survive. His brain was changing; his thoughts were being split in two. Now everything he knew was being reconsidered and divided into the human and animal position. And in the middle of his thoughts he felt something grow. It was only an idea, but he felt it like a tumor growing in his head. It was a switch. One side was marked MAN and the other was marked WOLF and he knew that all he had to do to flip it was decide which of the two he wanted to be. He kept it at MAN. He wasn't ready to handle the change just yet.

Suzie sat beside him. She hadn't experienced the agony that Bruce was suffering. She was born a werewolf, having inherited the condition from her father. She told him that it only lasted a few minutes, but truthfully she didn't know how long it would take before his pain ended and he could rise and stand strong against her father and anyone else who stood in his way.

"How are you doing?" she asked him gently.

"Fine," he mumbled. "Feel a bit...." He paused to think of the best word to describe the sensation his body was undergoing. "...weird."

Suzie kept her ears attuned to the woods that surrounded them, knowing that her father could jump out at them any second now.

"Could you hurry it up a bit?" she smiled in a way that suggested that she wasn't really kidding.

"I'll do my best," he promised before something that happened in his chest caused him to double over in pain. The pain was so intense he couldn't help but scream as it hit him. The sound of his cries started out sharp and shrill, but as they continued, they deepened in pitch and became more rounded and almost melodic. His screams became a howl that echoed deep throughout the forest.

"Well," Suzie said, "if Dad didn't know where we were before, he does now."

* * *

Mr. Greystone heard the howl and he stopped. He turned toward it and ran.

He was almost there. He was so close he could taste their flesh in his mouth. This was going to be quick, but it was going to feel so good.

* * *

Knowing that her father would be arriving soon, Suzie transformed back into her werewolf shape. She smelled him coming. He would be there in just a few minutes. She closed her eyes, calmed her heart and waited.

Bruce became quiet. The infection had done its job and he no longer felt any pain, but he was so exhausted that all he could do was close his eyes.

* * *

They were in the clearing. They were waiting to be slaughtered in the clearing. She was ready for him and her pathetic man was lying uselessly on the ground. This was going to be so easy.

* * *

She was ready for her father when he jumped out from the woods into the clearing. She easily dodged his swinging claws and turned around to cut into him with her own.

He howled in pain, and turned back and leaped on top of her. She fell on her back and kicked him off. He landed on his feet and jumped back on top of her, his razor sharp claws lunging her neck. She thrust her right arm up to block the move and he sunk his teeth into it. She howled in pain and tried to shake him off, but he would not let go. Not knowing what else to do, she lifted up her left hand and sunk one of its claws into his right eyeball. The howl that erupted from him was unlike anything she had ever heard. He let go of her arm and fell on his back as he held his hands to his wounded eye. She stood and panted uneasily, waiting for him to make the next move.

Already enraged past the point of insanity, her father went berserk. He lunged at her faster than he had ever moved before. His claws sliced into her before she could even react. He tore into her chest and her arms, hitting her so fast she fell to the ground in a heap. Standing over top of her, he raised his right arm and readied it for a final, deadly, swipe at her throat, but before he could deliver the *coup de grâce*, a hand grabbed his wrist and threw him to the ground.

Mr. Greystone looked up and saw Bruce standing over top of him.

"Sorry, Tony, but this is where the hunt has to end."

With that, Bruce tensed his body and did what his new instincts told him to do. Inside of him, he felt his bones move and grow. His muscles throbbed and grew strong. Hair sprouted from every available spot and his teeth and nails grew sharp and dangerous. His face changed. His eyes turned dark and his nose grew into a snout. His senses hit him in a way he had never felt before. He heard and smelled everything around him, especially Mr. Greystone's horrible stench. He felt stronger and faster than ever before, and just as Mr. Greystone jumped back up to attack him, his reflexes reacted before he even knew they were there.

He grabbed the older wolf by the throat and lifted him off of his feet. The muscles in his arm and hand twitched and tightened until Mr. Greystone's neck began to snap.

The old wolf fought against Bruce's grip, but it was too late. The last sound he heard was his own neck breaking in half. He went limp and Bruce dropped him to the ground.

Bruce transformed back into his human self and ran to Suzie, who was lying wounded on the ground. He took her back to the cabin, bandaged her wounds as best he could and drove her in her father's car to the closest hospital. He told the doctors an animal had attacked her and they believed him. They gave her a transfusion to make up for the blood she had lost and she stayed there for three days before they decided she was fit enough to go home.

While she recovered, Bruce went back to the woods where he had left Mr. Greystone's remains. There he found the broken body of a middle-aged man. He buried it, went back to the cabin and called a couple of tow trucks to retrieve the two damaged cars. He left Mr. Greystone's car at the cabin and caught a lift back with one of the tow truck drivers.

A week after Suzie got home, she and Bruce were visited by two police officers investigating the disappearance of her father. They told the investigators that they had gone out camping with Suzie's dad but left when she was wounded during a bear attack. Mr. Greystone had decided to stay put and the last time they had seen him, he was going out to find the bear that had attacked his daughter.

The two officers reacted skeptically to this story, but they had no evidence to disprove it. Mr. Greystone's body was not recovered and they reported that a wild animal attack was the most likely cause of his disappearance.

* * *

When it became clear that her father wasn't coming back, Suzie and Bruce got married. She took control of her father's company and put her new husband in charge of the day-to-day operations. Some of Bruce's former coworkers complained glibly that he had slept his way to the top, and they wondered how long it would be before he drove them out of business. But he proved them all wrong when he turned out to be even more ruthless and cutthroat in his dealings than his missing father-in-law had been.

As ruthless as he was, Bruce was surprised by how little effect his lycanthropic conversion had on his personality.

He still liked his meat well done, felt no compulsion to drink and enjoyed a nice salad with every meal. He realized that his late father-in-law's absurd machismo had nothing to do with being a werewolf, and this filled him with enormous relief. He never wanted to be as big a jackass as Tony Greystone.

Suzie was sitting beside him watching a movie on their couch when he had this little epiphany, and she noticed the content look on his face.

"What are you grinning about?" she asked.

"Nothing." He shook his head. "I was just thinking about something."

She smiled and leaned towards him and gave him a kiss. "I've been thinking about something too," she told him.

"Anything I should be aware of?" he asked.

Her smile deepened and tears of joy filled her eyes.

"Suzie? What is it?" he asked, surprised by her sudden emotional display.

"A couple of weeks ago I got a feeling I should go see a doctor or something," she explained. "I didn't get around to it until today..."

Bruce could see where this was going. He jumped off the couch, his body shaking with excitement. "Suzie? Are you—"

She nodded.

Bruce howled with joy. "For how long now?" he asked her.

"Six weeks," she told him.

He fell to his knees and hugged and kissed her stomach.

That night, as they lay in their bed, Bruce was still too excited to sleep. He thought about the girl—somehow he knew it was going to be girl—he would raise. He knew that she would be perfect. And when his perfect girl would become a perfect woman, any man who got close to her would have to prove that he was worthy. He would make sure of it.

The Living Dead

Roger didn't drink milk. He hadn't touched the stuff since he was a child. He hated the way it tasted, the way it smelled and especially where it came from. He couldn't understand how people were disgusted by the idea of drinking milk that had come from a dog or a baboon or any other animal, but they were perfectly okay with the stuff that came out of big, ugly dairy cow. The whole milk thing was a mystery to him.

Natalie, however, lived on milk, so as part of his duties as her husband, Roger stopped at the local convenience store every other evening to pick up a carton to take home. Over the two years they had been married, it had become such a large part of his routine that even when she went to visit her parents out of state, he would still pick up milk for her. He always ended up with a bunch of unopened cartons that he had to throw out before she got back, lest she think he was a crazy person.

So one night, like clockwork, he drove to the neighborhood Stop'n'Shop and parked his car in his usual spot, just as the sun started to set. He walked into the store, causing a small bell above his head to chime, announcing his presence.

"Hi Cedric," he called out to the young Chinese man who worked the store's night shift. Cedric didn't greet him back, which was unusual since he was habitually polite. Roger paused and saw that Cedric was not in his regular spot behind the counter. He looked around and noticed that he was the only person in the store.

"Hello!" he called out. "Anyone here?"

No one answered him.

With his eyebrows raised, he walked over to the store's back room, pausing to pick up a carton of milk along the way.

PARTLY SKIMMED
PARTLY SKIMMED MILK
1 LITRE

Placed at eye level on the door was a sign handwritten on a piece of cardboard that read "Employees Only." Roger, sensing something was wrong, decided to ignore this commandment and reached for the doorknob, only to find that it was locked. "Cedric? Are you in there?" he shouted through the door, earning only more silence for his efforts.

He scanned the store for clues that might prove that the suspicion that tingled through him was more than just his overexcited imagination. Nothing seemed to be out of place. Everything was where it should be. Except for Cedric. Roger frowned and walked over to the counter and took out his wallet, intending to pay for the milk, but he couldn't recall how much the carton cost—even though he had bought milk at least three times a week for the past two years. He would always just give Cedric a five and get back some change, which he would stuff, uncounted, into his jacket pocket.

Wondering what to do next, Roger noticed that the security camera in the far right-hand corner of the store wasn't plugged into the wall. Someone had obviously tampered with it. With the carton of milk still in his hand, he ran to the back room door and started pounding on it.

"Cedric!" he shouted. "Are you okay? Answer me!"

There was still no answer, so he sped to the phone on the front counter to call 911. He picked up the phone to dial when a loud shot echoed throughout the store and the phone just exploded into a hundred pieces. Several of these flying projectiles cut into Roger and he cried out in pain. He turned around and saw a small wiry man with a ski mask pulled over his head.

"Don't move!" the man hissed, his order backed up by the gun he held in his left hand.

Roger froze and instinctively raised his hands above his head. To his horror, Roger noticed the man was covered in blood, but he did not appear to be seriously hurt. The man was obviously frightened; he was perspiring heavily and his hands were shaking.

"You don't need that," Roger insisted, referring to the man's weapon. "I'm not going to hurt you."

"Shut up! Don't say another word!"

The two of them stood there silently for a few seconds, until the quiet was disturbed by the sound of a sneaker squeaking against the store's linoleum floor. Roger looked up and saw Cedric staggering out of the doorway to the back room. Weakened by the loss of blood, he appeared barely able to stand. When the gunman turned to see what was happening, Roger grabbed the closest thing to him—the milk carton—and threw it as hard as he could at the man, but he was too slow. The carton was only halfway through the air when the man—surprised by Roger's sudden movement—fired a shot into the air. The carton exploded as the bullet tore through it and the white liquid splashed onto the wall and floor. The small projectile continued on its path and hit Roger in the neck. A horrible gurgling sound bubbled through his throat as he fell to his knees. The gunman fired a shot into Cedric and then turned to fire two more shots at Roger. His body collapsed to the floor and the blood from his wounds flowed into the white milk.

* * *

PHHHHHHHIFFFFFFFFFFFFTTTTTTTTTT-SHUU-UUUUUUUU

PHHHHHHHIFFFFFFFFFFFFTTTTTTTTTT-SHUU-UUUUUUUU

PHHHHHHHIFFFFFFFFFFFFTTTTTTTTTT-SHUU-UUUUUUUU

The sound was steady and almost soothing in its unyielding rhythm. Roger couldn't remember when he had first noticed it, but he did know it was the first thing he *had* noticed since his last memory had ended and his new ones had begun. It was dark wherever he was. He didn't feel strong enough to speak, but that didn't seem to matter since—as far as he could tell—there wasn't anybody for him to talk to. He could feel a weight against his body, but he couldn't tell if he was standing or lying down. He tried to move, but his arms and legs refused to listen to his commands. After a while he gave up, since it made no sense to move around when he did not even know where he was. Wherever it was, he had been there for what seemed like months, but it could have easily just have been a few days or even hours. He tried counting the seconds, but he found it hard to concentrate and gave up after a minute or two. Finally he decided to just relax and focus on the one thing he knew was real. He listened to the sound and tried to discern some meaning from its slow and constant measure.

PHHHHHHHIFFFFFFFFFFFFTTTTTTTTTT-SHUU-UUUUUUUU

PHHHHHHHIFFFFFFFFFFFFTTTTTTTTTT-SHUU-UUUUUUUU

PHHHHHHHIFFFFFFFFFFFFTTTTTTTTTT-SHUU-UUUUUUUU

* * *

The voice was hoarse and raspy, but still tinged with the kind of cheerful lilt that indicated a certain amount of natural friendliness. Roger could barely make out what was said. The voice had to compete with the background sound, but eventually he was able to make it out.

"Hey, buddy," the voice urged him. "Quit being a lazy ass and get your bony butt out of bed!"

"Huh?" Roger responded, speaking for the first time since he found himself in the darkness.

"I said, get up!" the voice ordered him.

"Can't..." Roger mumbled. "Can't move... Too dark..."

"It ain't dark," answered the voice. "You just got your eyes closed. Open them up and you'll know where you are."

"But my eyes are open..." Roger protested.

"Just humor an old man, will you?" insisted the voice.

Roger frowned as he discovered with a shock that his eyes had been closed all along. The light hit hard and blinded him. In an instant his world of darkness was replaced by a world of harsh yellow brightness, which eventually faded to reveal the world he was used to calling reality.

He looked up and saw that the voice was connected to an older black man dressed in a white hospital gown. The man smiled at him and introduced himself.

"Thought I was never going to get through to you," he said, putting out his hand for Roger to shake. "I'm Tiberius, but all my friends call me Bert."

Still confused, Roger sat up and reached over and shook the man's hand. As he did, he looked down and saw something that made almost jump out of his skin. Even though he was definitely sitting up, his body appeared to still be lying down.

"What the hell!"

Bert laughed. "Weren't expecting to see that, were you?" he asked with a amused expression on his face.

"What—" Roger was stunned.

"Get out of bed," Bert told him, "and I'll explain everything. As well as I can, that is."

Shakily, Roger lifted himself off of the bed. He jumped down to the floor and turned around and saw himself lying in a hospital bed, connected to a host of beeping and twittering machines, the loudest of which was connected to his mouth and nose and made a sound he found intensely familiar. *Phhhhhhhhifffffffffttttttttttttt-shuuuuuuuuuu. Phhhhhhhhifffffffffttttttttttttt-shuuuuuuuuuu. Phhhhhhhhifffffffffttttttttttttt-shuuuuuuuuuu.*

Overwhelmed by what he saw, Roger tried to fight the anxiety rioting through him, but he couldn't. He just poured out a torrent of confused and powerfully felt curse words. Bert watched with a knowing smile on his face. He had done the same thing when he had found himself in Roger's perplexing situation. Eventually Roger grew quiet.

"What is going on?" he asked Bert after a very long moment of silence.

"The modern world," Bert answered cryptically.

"Huh?"

"The modern world is what is going on," Bert explained, "and we're the result."

Roger just stared at him.

"Y'see," Bert continued, "at any other time in the history of mankind we'd have already made our trip up to the bright white light and be getting reacquainted with all of our dead pets and relatives, but we live in the modern world, where even something as simple as death manages to get complicated." He paused and let the machine next to him fill in the silence with one of its *Phhhhhhhhiffffffffftttttttttttt-shuuuuu-uuuuus*. "As far as our brains our concerned, we're gone. We're dead. But thanks to these machines they got us hooked up to, our hearts keep on pumping and our lungs keep on breathing. Forget what you've learned from all of the horror shows you've seen, because the two of us are the real living dead. Our spirits have been freed from our bodies, but we can't go anywhere until our bodies die."

"We're dead?" asked Roger, not completely comprehending what Bert had told him.

Bert shook his head.

"We're very much alive, but *we should* be dead. Our bodies have no use for our spirits, but we can't move on until they decide to quit."

"We're ghosts?"

"Living ghosts is the way I figure it." Bert smiled and nodded. He was glad to see that Roger was catching on.

"Why don't they let us die?"

Bert shrugged. "I don't know about you, but my daughter is very religious and she ain't about to give this hospital permission to let her papa die before the Lord is through with him," he explained. "Is there anybody like that in your family?"

"My parents," Roger said. "They don't believe people should have any say about when a person dies. They would never let them pull the plug on me."

"Well then, it looks like the two of us might be here for awhile."

"Is there anybody else like us around here?"

"Not quite," said Bert. "We're the lucky ones."

"Lucky?"

Bert nodded. "C'mon," he said, walking towards the door to Roger's room, "I'll give you the tour and show you what I mean." When he came to the door, he walked right through it as if it wasn't there.

Roger stood stunned, not having been prepared to see that happen.

Bert poked his head through the door.

"Are you coming?" he asked.

Roger broke out of his daze and nodded and followed Bert out through the door.

* * *

"That's Dr. Namora," Bert told Roger as they walked past a small serious-looking woman in her mid-50s, "and that's Marjorie Klein, one of the night shift nurses."

As they walked, Bert was busy pointing out everyone who worked there. Roger couldn't keep up, and by the fifth doctor and seventh nurse, he stopped trying. It looked like every other hospital he had ever been in. He had always hated hospitals and had done everything he could to avoid them, and the irony of his current situation became more uncomfortably apparent with each step.

"Well, that's the staff," Bert concluded, "at least all of them that's working today."

"Uh-huh," agreed Roger, obviously lost in his thoughts.

"You haven't heard a single thing I said, have you?" asked Bert with a smile.

"I'm sorry," he apologized, "it's just a lot to take in right now."

"I know," said Bert. "I went through it too, but like I said before, we got it easy compared to others around here."

"What do you—" Roger started to ask, but he was interrupted when Bert gestured to him to stop talking. He followed Bert's gaze and saw a confused-looking girl walking through the hallway.

"It ain't right," said Bert. "It just ain't right."

"What?" asked Roger.

"The kids. It ain't right for them to be taken so soon."

With that said he walked over to the young girl, who looked to be around six or seven, and crouched down and smiled at her. "What's your name, sweetheart?" he asked.

She looked at him and thought for a moment about whether he was the kind of stranger she should talk to. "Wendy," she spoke softly after she decided he looked safe.

"How do you do, Wendy? My name is Tiberius, but folks like to call me Bert."

"Hi, Bert," she greeted him shyly.

"You look lost, Wendy. Do you know where you are?"

She shook her head and burst into tears.

"Now don't you cry," he whispered kindly. "I'll help you find your way back."

"You will?"

"Sure I will. Just grab my hand and I'll lead the way." He stood up and offered her his right hand and she grabbed it gratefully.

Curious, Roger followed them as they started walking down the corridor. It led down into an area that was closed off from the public. They all walked through the doors of a blocked-off section, and Roger heard orders being shouted out from a group of doctors and nurses fighting to save someone's life. When he got close to them, he saw that their patient was a young girl.

It was Wendy.

"Now here we are," Bert said. "This is where you ought to be."

She smiled at him as Bert lifted her up and placed her down inside her own body. He turned and started walking away and laughed happily when one of the nurses announced that they had a pulse. The little girl was going to make it.

Roger couldn't believe what he had just seen. "You saved her! You brought that girl back to life."

"I just helped a bit," Bert said. "And it doesn't always work," he explained. "Sometimes it's their time to go and there ain't nothing anyone can do about that."

"Do you do this for everybody?"

"The kids mostly. They get confused. Most adults figure out what's going on and find their own way back. Besides I've got more important things to do."

"Like what?"

"Come on," Bert said, walking on, "I'll show you."

Roger followed him and a few minutes later (it should have taken longer but it's amazing how much time is saved when walls are no longer a barrier), they were in a dark room occupied with a single patient.

"I told you we are the lucky ones, and we are. I want you to meet Cailey. She's a friend of mine."

They walked over to the woman in the bed. She was very thin and appeared to be around 19 or 20. She looked like she was sleeping.

"Shouldn't we let her rest?" asked Roger.

"Rest is the last thing this poor girl needs," said Bert. "Hi Cailey." He bent over and greeted her warmly.

What happened next made Roger worry that something was wrong with his eyes. He thought for a second that he was seeing double or something like it because he saw Cailey smile and open her eyes even though her body never moved and her eyes stayed closed. At once she appeared to be asleep and awake. It was only when she greeted Bert back that he realized that he was seeing her spirit moving inside her body.

"How you doing, sweetie?" asked Bert.

"I'm okay," she told him. "Who's that with you?"

"This is my new friend Roger," Bert said. "He's like me."

"Nice to meet you, Roger."

Roger tried to return her greeting, but found himself at a loss for words. "I'm sorry," he apologized, "I've just never seen anything like this before."

"Very few have," said Cailey.

"At least no one who could tell the world about it, in any case," Bert added.

"What am I seeing?" asked Roger.

"Cailey here is in a coma," Bert explained.

"I was in a car accident," she told him. "Hit by a drunk driver. He got out of his car without a scratch and paid a fine, and I ended up like this. I'm kind of hoping that he'll spend his next life as a barnacle or something equally alive but useless."

"People like Cailey are stuck in a bigger bind than guys like us could ever dream of," Bert told Roger. "Because our

5
4
3
2
1
NUMBER

brains are dead, we can leave our bodies and entertain ourselves anyway we can, but their brains have just been tricked into thinking they're dead, but their spirits know better. That means they can't move around like we can. They're stuck wherever they're put. They can see and hear everything that happens around them. They experience time just like everyone else does, but to the world, it just looks like they're sleeping."

"It sucks," Cailey said, quickly summing up the experience.

"Is everyone who's in a coma like this?"

"No," said Bert. "Some of them manage to convince themselves that they *are* sleeping and time manages to pass more quickly for them. They're the ones who wake up and are shocked to learn 10 years of their life have passed them by. Then there are the ones who go nuts and spend the whole time hallucinating. Some of them are lucky and spend the time in a happy fantasy world, while the others find themselves in their own worst nightmares. And then you got the normal ones like Cailey here who just wait patiently for the day when they wake up."

"Or die," added Cailey.

"Now I told you, I don't like you talking like that," Bert chastised her.

"It's okay, Bert," she said. "I'm not afraid of death. At this point I'll settle for anything."

"Just humor an old man, will you?" he said as he moved her hair out of her eyes.

"Okay," she agreed. "How's Maxwell?"

"I haven't gotten around to visit him just yet," said Bert. "Been too busy showing Roger the sights."

"Who's Maxwell?" asked Roger.

"An old fellow like me. He's been in a coma for nearly 25 years now."

"He's a hoot," said Cailey.

"You've met him?" asked Roger.

"Sure," she said. "Once a week they take the two of us out of our beds and put us in wheelchairs and let us sit in the garden outside. I don't think they could ever know how much those days mean to us."

"How was your mom today?" Bert asked.

"She was good. Kept the tears to a minimum. She only cried twice."

"Cailey's mother is a very sweet woman," Bert explained to Roger. "She comes in and visits her daughter every single day. She reads to her and fixes her hair and tells her what is happening with her family."

"Yeah, she's great," Cailey agreed. "I just wish she picked out books *I* would like."

"At least she visits," said Bert. "The only reason I'm still here is because of my daughter and she hasn't come to visit in six months."

Cailey smiled. "Now Bert," she teased, "that's not the *only* reason you're still here."

Somehow—despite the darkness of his skin—it was obvious that this made Bert blush.

He waved dismissively. "Go on now. You know I don't need to hear that again."

"Hear what?" asked Roger.

"Bert's probably told you his living ghost theory," said Cailey, "but I have a theory of my own about why he's here."

"What is it?"

"He's our guardian angel," she explained. "Have you had a chance to see any of the things he does for the people in this hospital?"

"I saw him save a girl."

"He does that all the time. He pretends he has nothing better to do, but I know better. I can think of plenty of people in his situation who wouldn't lift a finger to help anyone, much less come over and spend time with someone like me every day."

"You're embarrassing me," Bert mumbled shyly.

"I don't care," Cailey told him. "You're a being of pure good, Tiberius, and in my books that elevates you to angel status, no matter what your theory is."

Before Bert had a chance to argue, the light in Cailey's room turned on as a nurse joined them.

"Must be morning," said Cailey. "Time for my sponge bath."

"Which means it's time for us to go," said Bert. "A lady needs her privacy."

As the nurse made her preparations, Bert and Roger left the room.

"Now it's time for you to meet Maxwell," said Bert, "and Cailey wasn't kidding. He really is a hoot. He used to be a firefighter until a collapsing wall landed on his head and put him in here. He's been trapped inside that body of his for longer than Cailey's been alive, but you'd never know it. I've never met a more cheerful fellow in my entire life."

It took them just a few seconds to get to Maxwell's room, and as soon as they did, Bert shouted out a greeting to his old friend.

"Hey there, old timer! How's life in the fast lane?"

The smile on his face faded when his greeting went unreturned.

"Max? Are you all right?" he asked as he approached his friend's bed.

Roger moved with him and looked down at the old man in the bed. Expecting to see the same odd combination of unconscious body and conscious spirit he had just observed in Cailey's room, he was surprised to find that Maxwell's spirit was not at all evident. All he saw was a still—and apparently lifeless—body.

"Max? Max, are you all right?" Bert asked again.

There was no response.

"Max!" Bert shouted. "It's me, Bert! Where are you?"

"Bert..." Roger whispered sadly. "I don't think he's here anymore."

Bert tried to protest. "But—"

"He's gone," Roger continued. "Your friend is gone."

Tears began to well up out of Bert's eyes. "But you didn't even get a chance to meet him," he protested through his tears. "He was such a great guy."

"Think of it this way," Roger comforted him. "He's free. He's in a better place and he's free."

"You're right," Bert whispered sadly. "I'm just sad that he's gone, is all. I'm going to miss him."

Together the two of them stood there until the room's lights turned on, thanks to the same nurse who had interrupted their visit with Cailey. She went over to Maxwell and noticed something was wrong. Twenty minutes later, Roger and Bert watched as his body was covered with a sheet and wheeled away to the hospital's morgue.

"I guess that's what they call balance," Bert said with a sigh. "The same day I make a new friend, I lose an old one."

* * *

After they left Maxwell's room, Roger decided to excuse himself from Bert so he could have some time to himself to process everything he had learned in the past few hours. Bert understood what Roger was going through and told him that he was going to see Cailey to tell her about the passing of their friend.

Roger—having nowhere else to go—went back to the room where his body was being—for lack of better term—stored. He briefly considered attempting to go back into his body, but found he had no real desire to return to it, so he just stood there and listened to the artificial breaths of the machine that was keeping him alive.

Phhhhhhhhiffffffffftttttttttttt-shuuuuuuuuu. Phhhhhhhhiffffffffftttttttttttt-shuuuuuuuuu. Phhhhhhhhiffffffffftttttttttttt-shuuuuuuuuu.

He still found the sound comforting and closed his eyes and thought about nothing for a very long time. He only opened them when he heard someone come into his room.

It was Natalie. She looked very tired and almost indescribably sad. He felt very guilty when he realized that during all this time he had barely given her a second thought. He was not the only person whose life was changed forever by the bullets that had put him here.

He watched as she walked over and pulled up a chair to sit beside his body. She grabbed his hand and held it for a very long time.

Phhhhhhhifffffffffttttttttttttt-shuuuuuuuuu. Phhhhhhhifffffffffttttttttttttt-shuuuuuuuuu. Phhhhhhhifffffffffttttttttttttt-shuuuuuuuuu.

She let the machine sing its never-ending song before, finally, she began to speak. She took a long, deep breath, as if she had kept something inside and was afraid of what might happen once she let it all out. Tears filled her eyes. It was going to be the hardest thing she had ever done.

"I've been thinking about this a long time, Roger," she said. "I refused to accept what the doctors were telling me for so long, but now I know that they're right. You're never going to wake up. The only reason you're still alive is this awful machine they have you connected to. That's not the way it should be. You shouldn't be kept here because we can't let you go. I owe it to you to let you die, but your parents will never let that happen. They know full well you could be another 50 years like this and they couldn't care less. That's why I'm taking them to court. I hired a lawyer two days ago. He thinks we're going to win. They tell me you can't hear anything I say to you, but if you can, I hope you understand why I'm doing this."

"I do," he said, knowing she couldn't hear him.

* * *

Bert wasn't happy to hear the news, but he took it well. "I'm going to hate to see you go," he told Roger. "Especially so soon after we've gotten to know each other, but I'm sure glad I'm going to have you and Max to talk to when my turn finally comes. Let's go tell Cailey the good news."

The two of them walked over to Cailey's room and saw that she was not alone. An older woman was sitting by her bed, reading aloud from a cheap paperback romance novel.

"Oh, I'm sorry," Bert apologized. "I didn't know your mother was here. We'll leave you alone with her."

"Don't you dare," Cailey ordered them. "Do you have any idea how bad this book is? What are you two up to?"

"Celebrating," Bert told her.

"Really? What's the occasion?"

"Roger here is going to get his plug pulled."

"You're kidding," said Cailey. "When?"

"I don't know yet," Roger admitted.

"His wife is going to court," Bert explained.

Cailey laughed. "Then it could be a long celebration," she told them.

"Why do you say that?" asked Roger.

"Haven't you heard about other cases like this? There are people who have been in your condition for decades while their family fights over whether or not to flip the switch that's keeping them alive."

"Oh," said Roger. "I didn't know that."

As hard as he could, Bert couldn't keep his face from breaking out into an enormous grin.

"Hey Bert," Cailey teased him, "try not and look too happy about it."

"I'm sorry," Bert told Roger. "I know this must be disappointing to you and all, but I really do like having someone I can walk around with."

"Don't worry about it," Roger replied. "I understand."

From behind them, they heard the door open. A man in nurses' scrubs popped his head through the door and told Cailey's mom that visiting hours were over.

"He's new," said Bert. "Have you seen him before?" he asked Cailey.

"A couple of times," she told him. "He went out with Max and me the last time the two of us went out to the garden."

Cailey's mom gathered her things to go and left the three of them alone in the room.

"Thank God," Cailey sighed. "I thought she was never going to stop reading that book."

"It could be worse," Bert told her. "She could stop coming at all."

"I know, I know," Cailey agreed. "It's just that when she reads something like that to me, it proves that she has no idea who I am. Sure she comes in and visits me every day, but for all that she really knows about me, she might as well visit a complete stranger."

"I'm sure that's just as much your fault as it is hers," Bert scolded her gently.

"Yeah, you're right. But, hell, if I can't complain about crap like this, who can?"

"Good point," Bert and Roger both agreed.

* * *

A few hours later Bert decided he was going to learn all he could about the new nurse he had seen earlier in Cailey's room. He investigated every new person who joined the hospital's staff, partly out of curiosity, partly out of concern, but mostly because he usually had a lot of time to kill. He asked

Roger if he cared to join him, and—not having anything else to do—Roger said yes.

The first thing they had to do was find him, which wasn't as easy as it sounded. It was a big hospital and both of them only barely remembered what the man looked like. As they searched for him, they happened into a room where they both recognized the patient.

"It's Wendy." Bert smiled when he saw her. He walked over to her and frowned.

"What's the matter?" asked Roger.

"I was hoping she'd be doing better than this. At least she managed to convince herself that she is sleeping."

"Pardon?"

"Remember how I told you folks in comas react to their situation in different ways?"

"Yeah, now that you mention it."

"Poor thing could have ended up trapped in her own body like Cailey, but luckily for her, this just seems like one very long nap. I hope she wakes up from it soon."

Bert shook his head and walked out of the room. Roger followed him and the two of them continued on their search for the new nurse, but he was nowhere to be found. They turned around and started walking back to where they had started when they spotted the man walking out of Wendy's room.

"Gotcha." Bert grinned triumphantly.

Seeing him now in the full glare of the hospital's fluorescent bulbs, they saw that he was a thin man of medium height with short, dark hair and a thin mustache that was best described as unfortunate.

The two of them started following him as he continued on his rounds. He worked quietly and efficiently and treated the patients with care and respect. They were with him for half an hour when a nearby commotion drew their attention away from him. They heard the familiar sound of doctors and nurses attempting to resuscitate a patient. Bert started moving toward it and within a few seconds he realized where the sound was coming from.

"Wendy," he said as he started running her room.

Roger ran after him, but they both got there too late. As they passed through the door, it was all over. The doctors had given up what was a lost cause and named the time of death.

"Damn it!" Bert swore angrily, wishing he had the ability to punch or kick something. "It's just not right!"

Roger looked down at the floor and said nothing. He couldn't disagree.

* * *

"The thing about hospitals," Bert decided, "is that if you spend any time in them, you have to get used to death. If you can't do it, then you have no business being here. The problem," he sighed, "is what do you do when you can't get used to it, but you can't leave either. I don't know why it affects me so much. I 'm dead, at least technically, so you'd figure I'd be more at ease with the whole process. But I'm not. The whole system strikes me as useless and unnecessary, and they better have a good explanation for it all when my time finally comes, and I get to see where it all ends." He paused for a moment. "Were you a Catholic, Roger?" he then asked, somewhat out of the blue.

"Lapsed," Roger admitted. "I haven't been to church since I left home to go to college."

"Then you know about purgatory?"

"Yeah."

"Sometimes that's what I think this place is. And all we can do is wait out our time until someone decides we're ready to leave. Until they've decided we've been forgiven for what we've done."

"I don't think we did anything," said Roger. "We're just here because of bad luck."

Bert sighed. "In your case, maybe."

"What do you mean?" asked Roger.

Bert grew silent and stared down at the ground. "I never told you about my accident, did I?" he asked eventually.

"No, you've never mentioned it."

"I used to be a truck driver. Spent a lot of time on the road. More than I should. My last trip out I had been driving for 30 hours straight and I could barely see I was so tired, but I couldn't be late so I kept going, hoping another one of the pills I kept taking would keep me from falling asleep at the wheel. It didn't. I woke up to the sound of a car horn. Just in time for me to watch my truck smash into a minivan. It took less than a second, but in my mind it lasted for a lot longer than that. It was enough for me to see them in there—the mom and the dad and their two kids. The last thing I remember was me flying out my windshield. I don't know where I ended up after that. The next thing I knew I was hooked up to that damn machine, and I knew that it was my punishment for what I did. Cailey calls me an angel, but she wouldn't if she knew. I don't do what I do here because I'm a good person. I do it so someday I'll be forgiven, and whoever put me here will let me leave."

Roger began to say that he didn't think it mattered why Bert did what he did, that just doing it was enough to make him a good person, but he stopped when it became clear that Bert had no desire to hear it.

* * *

Bert wanted to be alone, so Roger decided to go over and visit Cailey. As he got to her room, he was slightly surprised to see the nurse they had spent the day searching for walking out of it.

His shift should have been over a few hours ago, he thought. *Must be pulling a double*, he decided before he passed through Cailey's door and greeted her with a quick "hello."

She didn't greet him back.

"Cailey?"

Nothing.

He walked over to her. Her spirit was gone. Only her body remained.

Cailey was dead.

* * *

It took two hours before anyone else discovered Cailey's passing. Roger stood there and waited as they rolled her out, knowing that Bert would soon arrive and need to be told.

He was alone in the room for another hour before Bert finally came.

"Where's Cailey?" he asked immediately, even though the answer was evident in Roger's face.

"She's gone, Bert," Roger told him.

Bert stayed quiet. He had no more tears left to cry. A part of him even felt relieved.

"At least she's free," he whispered.

"Bert..." Roger spoke after he let this sentiment have its moment. "I'm not sure this was supposed to happen this way."

"What do you mean?"

"Remember that new nurse we were following around today?"

"Yeah, of course I do. Why?"

"I saw him leave here just before I went in."

"What are you saying?" Bert's face turned grim.

"It's just too much of coincidence. First Maxwell, then Wendy and now Cailey. He had contact with all of them and we know he was in both Wendy's and Cailey's rooms before they died."

Bert knew what Roger was thinking.

"I don't think…" Roger paused, pained by what he was about to say. "I don't think they died naturally. I think he murdered them."

"Why?" Bert looked down at the floor and whispered, "Why would he do that? All of them were already so close to death."

"I think that's exactly why he does it. This way he can feel the sick thrill of ending another person's life, knowing that no one will ever suspect him. Or maybe he thinks what he's doing is noble. Maybe he thinks he's ending their misery."

"It's not right!" Bert said angrily. "They weren't like the two of us. They could have woken up someday. The odds were against it, but it could have happened. But not anymore. Now they're all gone." Once again he cursed his inability to grab something and throw it across the room. "We have to stop him. This can't happen again."

"How?" asked Roger. "Neither of us can be seen or heard or affect the physical world in any way. There is nothing we can do."

"I won't accept that," answered Bert. "There must be something we can do to stop this. I refuse to believe that whoever is responsible for us being here would be so cruel as to make us watch this happen and not allow us to do anything about it. There must be a way."

"And if there isn't?"

"Then this isn't purgatory," Bert answered him. "This is hell."

* * *

Weeks passed and more patients died. Roger and Bert watched helplessly as the man, whose named they learned was Levi Domsky, went on his rounds and killed anyone whose sudden death would not be questioned. During all that time they could not think of a single way to stop him.

There had been days when they had followed the madman and watched as he ended another life. Bert became obsessed with the idea of stopping these horrible crimes, but his obsession yielded no solutions and the torment was almost too much for him to bear. He stopped watching Levi and stayed more and more in his own room.

Roger worried about what was happening to Bert, but he couldn't help but wonder if it was a far saner reaction than his own. He had chosen to continue following Levi, even though he knew it was a futile mission. He hoped that maybe someday, when he had finally passed, there would be a reckoning in Levi's future, and he would serve as a witness to the man's crimes.

Roger had grown so used to the idea that the two of them were unable to affect Levi in any way, that a part of him came to believe that it also worked the other way. But then—one quiet night—he realized he had been wrong. Very wrong.

It took him a second to even realize what was happening. Levi walked into a room and found an old black man hooked up to a machine that was keeping him alive.

"Bert!" Roger shouted as he ran into the room.

Bert was watching when Levi walked over to the machine and casually flipped a switch.

It stopped.

Bert and Roger watched helplessly as Bert's body began to die.

"I didn't think it would be like this," Bert told Roger.

"It ain't right," Roger said sadly.

"I suppose I should be happy. I've been looking forward to this for so long. But not now. Not this way."

"I'm sorry, Bert," Roger said with tears in his eyes.

"It isn't your fault," Bert said shaking his head. "I should have thought of something. I just couldn't figure it out." He looked down sadly at his dying body and slowly began to fade away. As his spirit grew weaker, his look of sadness was replaced by one of horror. "Not now!" he cried out. "Not now!"

"What is it?" asked Roger, barely able to make out Bert's shape in front of him.

"I know how to stop him! I know—"

Bert was gone.

Levi checked the body for a pulse and made sure that it was dead. When he was certain, he went back to the machine and turned it back on. He then slipped out of the room. No one saw him come in and no one saw him leave. Bert's death would not be questioned.

* * *

Bert couldn't believe his eyes. He was dead, he knew that for sure, but he hadn't gone anywhere. As far as he was concerned he was still standing in his hospital room, but it wasn't like before. Roger couldn't see him. He shouted out to him, telling him the answer they had been searching for, but he couldn't be heard.

From behind him he felt the presence of another person. He turned and saw a man in a white suit.

"Tiberius Washington?" asked the man, who spoke with a slightly artificial English accent.

"Yes."

"My card," the man handed him a simple white business card that Bert read.

"Angel of Death?"

"That's right," answered the man. "I've come to take you to the judgment place."

"I can't go," Bert insisted. "Not without telling Roger what he has to do."

"I'm afraid you must," said the man. "It's your time to go."

"No," Bert said, shaking his head. "Not with that crazy man out there. I won't go."

"I'm sorry, Mr. Washington, but the concerns of the world you have left are no longer yours to worry about. You have bigger fish to fry."

"Listen to me!" shouted Bert as he grabbed the man by the lapels of his jacket and shook him. "I am not leaving!"

"I don't have time for this!" the man shouted back. "I'm behind schedule and I have to be in L.A. in 10 minutes!"

"I don't care," Bert hissed.

"Fine!" The man pushed Bert away from him. "Do you want to know what happens to people who refuse to meet their judgment? They stay where they are! Forever. If you don't go with me now, then you will be left here for the rest of eternity. Now think about it. Is this where you want to be for as long as this universe exists?"

Bert didn't even hesitate. "Yes," he said.

"Your funeral," the man said before he faded out of sight, presumably on his way to Los Angeles.

* * *

Bert found himself alone in his room with his dead body. Roger was gone. Standing there, Bert felt different than he had before. Before he had died, he had felt connected to something, but now that connection was gone. It didn't feel like he had been freed from anything. Instead it felt like the rope that kept him safely tethered to the ground had been cut, and he was now forced to go wherever the wind blew him. He closed his eyes for just a second, and when he opened them, his body was gone. He watched as people moved and faded in front of him, as hours and days skipped and jumped around him. No longer anchored to the realities of the living world, his spirit was now displaced in time. Just when he thought he had it all figured out, it changed again and the world slowed to an infinitesimal crawl. He spent what felt like a week inside of a single second.

Whenever he tried to go somewhere specific, he would end up someplace else. He found that if he tried hard enough he could have a small effect on the world around him. If he said something, someone might hear it—often mistaking it for a thought of their own. Occasionally he would touch something and it would move. He now had the power to do something to stop Levi, but whenever he got close to the man, he would find himself instantly transported to another room, as if the murderer was being protected by something far bigger and important.

He saw Roger all of the time, but was never able to talk to him.

What felt like years passed, and Levi's body count grew to an unimaginable number. There were times when it seemed like he was on the verge of being caught, but it never happened—as if the thing that was protecting him from Bert was also protecting him from capture.

Then, one day, time turned back to normal, or if not normal, then—at least—how Bert remembered it.

He looked around and saw that he was in Roger's room. Both Rogers were there, the spirit and the body. The body looked older by about 10 years. The spirit was the same. They weren't alone. Doctors were with them, along with a small woman with dark hair who must have been Roger's wife, Natalie.

It took Bert a second to realize what was happening. After a decade, she had won her case. She was there to turn off the machine and let her husband go.

Bert knew this was it. This was the moment he had been waiting for!

"Roger," he spoke as he ran after his friend's spirit. "You have to hear me! Now more than ever, you have to hear me."

His friend did not hear him. Instead he just watched as his wife said a prayer and nodded to the doctor who was standing beside the machine.

"Roger!" Bert pleaded. "This is it! We have no more time! If it doesn't happen now it never will!"

Roger turned his head for a moment, as if he were distracted by a sudden voice that appeared in his head.

"That's it, Roger! Listen to me! I'm right here!"

"Bert?" Roger asked aloud.

"It's me, buddy! Now listen, we don't have any time. You have to get back into your body before it dies. That's how we can stop Levi!"

"What good will that do?" asked Roger.

"Nothing. It's what you do after that that counts!"

"What?"

"Live!"

"I don't understand?"

"It's simple. Just live. That's all you have to do. Just wake up and live."

"But I can't."

"Who says so? Miracles happen, buddy, and if this isn't the time and place for one, then I don't know when is."

Roger turned his head and couldn't believe his eyes.

"Bert," he said. "I can see you."

"You're fading away, Roger! You have to do it now! You have to live!" Bert shouted at him.

Roger nodded and walked over to his body and laid down.

Natalie and the doctors watched as the man in front of them slowly succumbed to the injuries he had suffered more than a decade before. She didn't bother wiping away the tears that were streaming down her face.

Roger felt himself fading away, felt his spirit being pulled to somewhere else, but he fought against it and did what Bert had told him to do. He fought against death and refused to let it take him away. He ignored everything he knew about the natural world and the laws of science and did the one thing he had absolutely no right to do.

He lived.

He was so weak he couldn't move, but he had never before felt so strong. With every ounce of strength he had, Roger opened his eyes and looked out at the people around him.

The doctors gasped with amazement. Natalie fainted away.

* * *

Roger's recovery was slow. Agonizingly slow. His muscles had atrophied to the point that he would never walk again, even after extensive therapy. It took him months to get his voice back, but once he did he started saying things to the nurses. Things that made them suspicious of the man named Levi. They started watching him, and one night he was caught holding a pillow over an old man's face. He was arrested and eventually confessed to causing the deaths of 83 patients over the last 10 years. He received a life sentence for every person he killed, but died within six months of his imprisonment. His cellmate didn't like how he snored at night and made sure he never did it again.

Eventually Roger got out of the hospital and moved back in with Natalie. The two continued on with their lives. She still drank lots of milk, but he no longer had to get it for her.

And just as the man in white had warned him, Bert remained at the hospital. Before he had felt that the building was a purgatory, but he now knew it was where he was truly meant to be.

He never once regretted his decision to stay.

Samantha's Diary

WARNING!

This diary is the personal private property of the spirit of Samantha Louise Dexter (age 16¾) and is NOT meant for the nosy, prying eyes of anyone foolish enough to open it and read it without her express written permission (which she will never EVER give to anyone—EVER!) If she catches you with it, you WILL suffer torments the likes of which the living has never known!

That's a promise!

October 25, 2000
Dear Diary,
Today was my funeral. It was pretty cool. A lot of people were there! Like maybe 200 or even more! I didn't think I even knew that many people. Unfortunately, one of the people there was that two-faced cow, Jenny Beiderman. I hate her so much! You wouldn't believe how she was hanging on to Aidan and crying on his shoulder. I've barely been dead a week and already she's making a move on my boyfriend! Yeah, she was crying all right, crying tears of happiness. She knows that with me gone, she's a shoe-in for Prom Queen, but I'll show her. I bet you anything that in this year's yearbook she'll get one little picture of her and her pathetic crown stuck in the back corner of a page no one will ever look at, while I'll get a full page devoted to me at the front. I just hope they don't use the same picture that was on my school I.D. I'd hate to be remembered as the dead girl with the big honking zit in the middle of her forehead.

My dad gave my eulogy and it was *soooo* sad. I just wish he hadn't worn that dorky suit. He's had that thing since I was a baby! You'd think he'd be willing to buy a new one for the funeral of his only daughter. He broke down a couple of times and blamed himself for what happened, which isn't fair. I begged him to let me get that nose job. It isn't his fault the anesthesiologist was a drunk who gave me too much gas and put me into that coma. I just hope he buys a new suit with the money they'll get in the lawsuit against the hospital.

Mom looked gorgeous. She got her hair streaked and it looks awesome! You should have seen it when Jenny's mom went over to talk to her. It was hilarious! Mrs. Beiderman is actually a year younger than my mom, but she looks at least 20 years older! If Jenny had any shame, she'd take her mom directly to a Pilates class and a weight-loss clinic. They say that girls grow up to look just like their mothers, so Jenny better spend as much time with Aidan as she can now because in 20 years, she's going to look like her grandmother.

Joe came in from college. He looked really sad. The two of us never had much in common, so it was nice to see him so shaken-up by the death of his little sister. I was so proud of him when Jenny tried to give him a big hug and he just gave her a quick pat on the back before he pushed her away. He knows a phony when he sees one.

It was really weird being there, watching it all. I knew that none of them could see or hear me (even when Jenny got up to say something and I started gagging), but it felt like they knew I was there. Maybe they did.

When it was over, everyone came back to the house for pie. My parents had ordered 50 lemon meringue pies from Luigi's Bakery because they knew it was my favorite dessert in the world. It was torture watching everyone eat. Because of my stupid diet, I hadn't had a slice since my 14th birthday, and now that I don't have to worry about my weight, I can't eat anything! What a gyp!

I overheard my dad talking to one of his friends and it turns out I wasn't even in the casket they buried. Can you believe that! He said they had decided to donate my organs to people who needed transplants and stuff. At first, I got really mad when I heard him. It's not like they asked my permission and they know how I don't like strangers touching my stuff!! But then he said that my heart had gone to a girl my age who had been on the waiting list for four years, and I realized that she probably needed it a lot more than I did. I hope she likes it.

I'm back in my room now. My mom hasn't let anyone in here since they pulled the plug on me. It's going to be a shock to their system when they find out I left a half-eaten tuna fish sandwich on my desk. Luckily, I have no sense of smell, so I can't inhale the toxic stench of that sewage waste Jenny seems to think is perfume. God, I hate her!

October 31, 2000
Halloween
Dear Diary,
It's been a pretty quiet week, which is why I haven't written anything since my last entry. There's not much to do when you're dead, except watch the living and that gets really boring after a couple of hours. Joe went back to school and now it's just my parents in the house and they're still acting like zombies because of all the grief and stuff. It's weird, because it's not like they ever paid that much attention to me when I

was alive, so I don't know why they're so unhappy that I'm gone. I know they loved me, but when I think about the past three years or so, I can't really think of anything we ever did together, not counting Christmas, Thanksgiving and the Super Bowl. Dad spent all of his time at work, doing whatever he does at that company whose name I still can't pronounce. Mom was always at the gym or taking a class in something stupid, and I was busy with school and hanging out with Aidan and that bimbo Jenny Beiderman (I HATE HER!! Why was I ever friends with her? I must have been mental!).

Things wouldn't be so bad if Mom and Dad knew how to have a good time. All Dad does when he gets home is sit in front of the TV and watch the news. He doesn't even pick up the remote! He just leaves it on one channel and keeps watching it, even during the commercials. I scream at him to turn it to MTV or *Friends* or anything good, but he can't hear me and I end up watching all this really boring stuff about politics and junk. I guess there's an election coming up next month. I was going to run for student body president this year, and I would have won too because the only person who would have gone up against me was that weird girl with the dreadlocks and army boots who was always pushing those dumb petitions.

My mom is even worse because all she does when she gets home is sit down and read those stupid self-help books. When I can't stand watching the news with dad anymore, I'll read them by looking over her shoulder. Her latest one is a whacko diet book that's all about how evil carbohydrates are. It's crazy! There's no way she could ever follow it. The last time she tried to cook red meat, she started to cry and insisted that from that point on, she would only cook animals that were ugly or brainless, like fish and chicken. She is looking good, though. Mourning suits her. I'm just afraid that all of her crying is going to put bags under her eyes, and after what happened to me, she might be hesitant about getting surgery.

Today is Halloween. Last year me and Jenny (HATE HER!) dressed up like those trailer trash girls on Jerry Springer and we went trick-or-treating. Some people grumbled at us for being too old, but it was still a lot of fun. I ended up giving all of my candy to Aidan because there was no way my waistline could handle that much sugar. Today I spent three hours standing by the door while my parents handed out treats. It was the first time I saw them smile since you-know-what. They really went all out this year and handed out full-size candy bars and not those dinky little ones most people give.

A couple of the kids were dressed as zombies and ghosts, and it was funny to see how they all got it wrong. I don't look anything like that. At least I hope I don't. Come to think of it, I have no idea what I look like. I suppose it's possible that I'm all gross and scary and just don't know it. Or maybe I don't look like anything. I am invisible, after all. As usual, my mom dressed up as Catwoman, which got her some dirty looks from kids' moms and smiles from their dads. My dad just wore sweat pants and a T-shirt. He's starting to get a bit doughy. I think Mom should get him on a workout routine before he gets too gross.

November 20, 2000
Dear Diary,
Not much to report, Diary. I'm happy to say that Mom managed to get over her fear of plastic surgery and had those

injections put into her face. I can't remember what they're called but it starts with a "b." Whatever they are, they freeze her face and stop her from getting wrinkles, which is great, and now I don't have to feel guilty about what all that crying did to her face.

Dad was obsessed with the news before, but you should see him now. It's insane. I guess something funny happened with the election and they still don't know who is going to be president. Can you believe that? I was involved in every student election since grade seven and we never once had to have a recount. It's not like it's rocket science or anything.

December 7, 2000
Dear Diary,
It's been close to two months since anyone has come into my room. That sandwich must really be starting to reek. You'd think they'd smell it through the door by now.

December 18, 2000
Dear Diary,
Joe came home for Christmas vacation. He looks good and tanned. That Californian sun is doing wonders for his complexion. He brought his girlfriend with him. She seems real nice, but is kinda dumb. My mom tried to talk to her about an article on the latest trends in handbags in the new issue of *Vogue*, but Nicole (that's her name) hadn't even read it! Who doesn't read *Vogue*? Then my dad asked her what she was studying at school and she said she's studying English. What a waste of time! He asked her what she planned to do with her degree, and she said she didn't know. Then what's the point, right? I don't get it. Joe's really smart so I don't know

what he would see in someone who is studying a language she already understands and who isn't smart enough to know that people only go to school so they can make a lot of money when they graduate.

Still I have to give Joe some credit. The first thing he did when he got home was complain about the smell coming from my room. He wasn't there five minutes before he walked in and threw away the rotting tuna fish sandwich. You should have seen the look on his face! It was hilarious! I thought he was going to pass out. It must have really stunk!

December 23, 2000
Dear Diary,
Today ended up being a hard day for Mom. Dad and Joe were out getting a tree and she and Nicole were going through the boxes filled with Christmas decorations. She was fine at first, but then she found the stocking with my name on it that my grandmother gave me when I was baby. She lost it big time and started to cry. Nicole just hugged my mom until she was okay again. I think maybe I underestimated Nicole. She might be good enough for Joe after all.

December 25, 2000
Dear Diary,
I must admit I was a little jealous watching everybody open their presents, knowing that none of them were for me. Still I felt bad because I could tell that the smiles on their faces were a bit forced (especially Mom's since that stuff in her face makes it really tough to express any kind of happiness). I think they felt guilty celebrating without me, and they shouldn't. Unfortunately, that's the type of thing the living

can't understand. This whole death thing only makes sense when you're dead, which seems a bit ass-backwards to me. Wouldn't people enjoy their lives more if they weren't so afraid of what could happen to them after death? I don't get why there has to be all this secrecy about everything. Sure, things have been pretty dull since I died, but the truth is they weren't very exciting when I was alive. I don't think they would be so sad if they knew I was with them in spirit.

January 1, 2001
New Year's Day
Dear Diary,
Happy New Year! Sorta... The truth is, Diary, when you're a shapeless invisible spirit with nothing but time on your hands, things like dates and years don't mean very much. Days especially don't mean anything to me anymore. I don't sleep or go to school or do anything that might make one day different from the next. The only way I manage to keep track is by watching my parents. If they sleep in, I know it's the weekend. Some days are a lot easier to keep track of than others. Holidays obviously are the easiest to recognize.

Yesterday was New Year's Eve and I could tell because of all of the preparations my parents were making. You see, they've always had a New Year's Eve party at the house. It's a tradition. For the past 20 years their friends haven't had to worry about how they would celebrate the New Year. I guess this year was the first time this was ever in doubt, but my mom called to let everyone know the party was going to go ahead as usual, which made me happy. I would hate it if my death kept my parents from celebrating their favorite day of the year.

The house looked great. Dad was drunk by the time the third couple arrived. Mom looked beyond fantastic. She had on this red cocktail dress that looked elegant and sexy at the same time. She looked like a movie star! It was funny because no one mentioned me, but I could tell I was definitely in their heads. Everyone had a good time, but it was different than it usually was. It was as if everyone had been invited to a make-out party at a real popular kid's house, but when his parents refused to leave the basement, everyone sort of sat there and tried not to look stupid. I went to my room and left them all alone for a while, but when I came back, things still felt the same. My parents still managed to have a good time, so I guess it worked out okay.

February 2, 2001
Dear Diary,
My parents are acting weird. A few weeks ago, I noticed that they weren't talking to each other. But it's not like they had a fight or were mad at each other. They just don't speak. Mom comes home and makes dinner (she's actually started to cook red meat again) and they sit at the table and eat without saying a word. Then Dad gets up and cleans the table and does the dishes like he always does, and Mom goes into their room, reads or sits at my old computer (which they took out of my room last month and put in the basement) and logs onto the Internet. My dad watches the news or one of those mega-boring shows about World War II they always show on cable. After a few hours, they get up and go to bed. They don't say goodnight to each other or anything. They just go to sleep. The only time they hear each other's voices is when Joe calls and they both talk to him on the phone. Even then

they really only talk to Joe, but since they're on the same phone line, it's impossible for them to avoid hearing each other.

What is wrong? Why are they acting like this? Is it because of me? They seemed like they were doing better. They had so much fun at their New Year's party, but now it seems like they don't know what fun is anymore.

Oh, yeah. Today would have been my birthday. Truth is, the day seems meaningless when you know you aren't going to get any presents.

March 15, 2001
Dear Diary,
Remember when I wrote that my parent's weren't speaking to each other? Those are now officially the good old days. Now all they do is fight and scream at each other. They do it over everything. Tonight, Dad was mad because of my mom's weirdo diet. She had stopped buying any kind of bread.

"How am I supposed to make a (bleeping) sandwich if there's no (bleeping) bread in the house?" was how he put it.

Mom responded by saying, "Listen Tubby, the last thing you need is another meal."

It got pretty bad after that. Sometimes they get so mad I think they're going to hit each other, which makes me feel afraid for my dad 'cause my mom would seriously kick his ass. She works out seven days a week and could easily take him down without breaking a sweat, while he would be lucky to get one punch in before he dropped dead of a heart attack.

They are only civil together when Joe calls. Then they become all sweet and nice, and pretend they weren't shredding each other up just a minute ago.

I used to hate it when they were gone, but now I look forward to it every day. As boring as it is, it sure beats watching the two people you love more than anything hate each other.

April 26, 2001
Dear Diary,
Mom and Dad just got back from California, where they attended Joe's graduation. I wonder how they acted in front of him. Did they pretend to be nice to each other? I hope so. Dad wasn't back for ten minutes before he started calling people and bragging about the big impressive job Joe got with a company in New York. It's been a long time since I heard that kind of pride in his voice.

May 13, 2001
Dear Diary,
I don't know where to begin! I'm still in shock and can't really believe it happened, but it did. I know it did! I know it!

Since I last wrote, my parent's fighting has gotten even worse. Now they can't even look at each other without arguing. Two weeks ago I caught my dad on the phone talking to a lawyer friend of his when mom was out taking a pottery class. He asked the guy what would happen if he tried to get a divorce, and he learned that Mom would get half of everything, so he decided it wasn't worth it and told his friend that he would try and patch things up with her. What he didn't know was that Mom was also talking to her friends, and when she learned that she would end up with half of everything, she decided it was worth it. Ever since then, she's become so cruel and evil, I don't even recognize her. Dad made a few attempts to win her back and she shot him down so hard.

It was horrible. I can't stand to see them act like this. I mean, I HATE Jenny Beiderman, but I would still treat her better than how my parents are treating each other. So, today they were having the biggest fight ever. I don't know how it started—they were already at each other's throats when I came into the living room.

It turns out Mom was mad because Dad used a significant part of their life savings to buy stock in some company from Texas, and its price had been on a slow decline ever since. She wanted him to sell his shares before all of the money he invested was gone and he refused, insisting the company was going to bounce back within the next month or two.

"If this is about your stupid pride, is it worth putting us in the poor house?" she shouted.

"Ha!" he laughed. "Like you would stay with me if the money was gone! The minute I become poor, you'll find yourself another sucker to leech on to!"

"When I think of all the things I've given—" she started.

"Given?" he interrupted. "What have you ever given me besides credit card statements and veiled insults about my weight?"

"I gave you a son and a daughter and a home!" she shouted back at him.

"Yeah, what a good job you did with Samantha," he snorted. "Why do you think she wanted that surgery? I'll tell you why! Because her own mother couldn't ever let her forget how much prettier she would be if she didn't have that bump on her nose! She didn't have a (bleeping) bump on her nose! You just couldn't stand the fact that she was growing up to be more beautiful than—"

"STOP IT!!!!!!"

My dad stopped. He just stared at my mom, unable to believe what he had just heard.

It was me.

I screamed at him—at both of them—and they heard me! They heard me! I was there and I screamed at them and they heard me! Can you believe it? Because I'm not sure if I do. Maybe my dad just stopped because he knew he had gone too far.

Maybe.

I've got to find out for sure.

May 26, 2001
Dear Diary,
My parents have stopped fighting since the "incident" a couple of weeks ago, but that doesn't mean things have gotten any better. My mom and dad seriously seem to hate each other and I can't understand why.

Okay, so it wasn't like theirs was a love for the ages, or even like a Jennifer Lopez movie, but at one point it was real. It did exist. And the only thing that has seriously changed since then was what happened to me and I can't see how it could have driven them apart. I mean, isn't a tragedy supposed to bring people together? The way they talk to each other, it's like they never felt anything for each other, as if the years they spent together, when I was alive, weren't real.

I've tried everything since that last argument to get their attention once again, but it's no use. I think that night was a fluke. Maybe I can't force it to happen again. Or maybe the two of them have just become so distant that they can't hear me no matter how loud I am.

And, by the way, Dad was wrong about why I wanted to get that nose job. It's true that Mom always did talk about it having a bump, but that isn't why I did it. I begged my dad to let me get the operation because Aidan had told me that he thought Jenny had a cute little nose. He didn't say it to make me jealous or anything. Jenny did have a cute little nose, and after he pointed it out, I wanted it for myself. As much as I may want to blame him and (especially) Jenny, I know I'm the only person (besides that stupid anesthesiologist) responsible for what happened to me. I just wish there was a way I could tell them that.

June 9, 2001
Dear Diary,
Dad left the house last week and he hasn't been back since. He left because one night Mom didn't come home. He asked her where she had been and she refused to tell him, but he knew. He asked her who it was, but she just stared at him like he wasn't even worth her contempt.

Since then she's hardly been at the house. At first it felt like a relief to have them both gone, but now the house has become so quiet and lonely (and boring!) that I think I'm going to lose it. Yesterday, it got so bad, I was five minutes away from making the walls bleed (assuming that I could—I haven't really tried).

Mom hasn't even heard the message Joe left yesterday on the phone. He's been calling for the past couple of days, but since she's never here to answer him, he decided to tell her his big news on the machine. He's getting married! Can you believe it? He proposed to that Nicole girl he brought home for Christmas and she said yes!

The wedding is going to be in November. I wish I could be there. Maybe something like this could get my parents back together. I know they haven't told Joe that they're separated. Chances are they'll go to the wedding together, and maybe seeing Joe and Nicole will remind them of what they once had. I know it's a stupid thought, Diary, but right now it's all I've got.

July 17, 2001
Dear Diary,
My mom was going through her mail today when she came upon a letter that was addressed to her and Dad. I didn't recognize the name on the return address, but my mom must have because she tore into the envelope as quickly as she could. Inside it was a photograph and a short handwritten note that made my mom cry as soon as she started reading it. She was shaking so hard that I had to wait until she put the note down before I could see what it said.

> Dear Mr. and Mrs. Dexter:
> My name is Tonikka Benson and I wanted to write to you because I'm the girl who was given your daughter Samantha's heart. I cannot imagine how difficult it must have been for you to make that decision so soon after her death, but I can tell you what a difference it has made in my life. Before the transplant I was so weak I couldn't even leave my bed. I couldn't go outside or go to school or do much of anything. Thanks to your incredible gift, I am no longer a prisoner in my room. For the first time in my life I am free! I can go anywhere and do things I used to only dream about.

Next September I am going to start going to a real school with other kids! And I've included a picture of me that was taken last week during my very first camping trip! I am sure that you are still very sad your daughter is no longer with you, but I hope your grief will ease just a little with the knowledge that I would not be writing this letter to you if it weren't for her. Without her heart, I would not be starting a normal life.

Thank you,
Tonikka Benson

After I finished reading it, I looked down at Tonikka's picture and saw a petite girl close to my age sitting in front of a tent in the woods. On her face was the widest smile I had ever seen. On most people that smile would look fake or posed, but on her it was obviously the real thing. I have never seen someone so happy. That smile existed because of me!

I don't care what happens now. I don't care if my parents get divorced or if I end up spending the rest of eternity alone in this stupid house. For that smile it was worth it.

July 31, 2001
Dear Diary,
Mom was screaming at Dad over the phone today. I guess he's still holding onto that stock even though it keeps going down in price. I think she's afraid that by the time she divorces him, he'll have nothing left to take.

I hope the stupid company (I think it starts with an "e") goes bankrupt and Dad loses everything. The way the two of them have been acting, they deserve to be poor.

August 17, 2001
Dear Diary,
It finally happened again!
For the past couple months I've known that my mom has been seeing some other guy, but today she brought him over to the house for the very first time. Like I expected, he's really tall and handsome, and he came in wearing a gorgeous suit. His hair was dark and perfect and looked like it belonged on a superhero. I hated him immediately. It's so unfair of Mom to make Dad compete with a guy who barely seems human. He's the type of guy who usually only exists in razorblade commercials.

His name is Rance. No lie, that's his actual name. Can you believe it? Rance! What kind of name is Rance? As soon as he walked into the house, he had this sneer on his face.

"So are these your kids?" he asked my mom as he looked at the family photograph we posed for just a month before I died.

"Yes," she smiled. "That's Joseph." She pointed to my brother. "And that's Samantha."

"Is she the one who died?" he asked blankly.

My mom just nodded.

And then he said, "Too bad. She would have been a real looker in a few more years."

WHAT A CREEP! What kind of guy tells the woman he's dating that her dead daughter was on her way to being a hottie? And what does he mean "would have been"? I've seen that photograph a billion times and I can say with 100% certainty that in it I already look more beautiful and mature than any woman this sleazoid ever dated (except my mom). What does she see in him?

Then he said something really cheesy like "C'mon over here, baby" and they started kissing. I couldn't take it! Nothing could prepare me for this. I didn't know what else to do to make them stop, so I reached for the object closest to me. I could actually feel the picture frame in my hand as I held it! It's been close to a year since I've felt anything!

I slammed the photo against the wall near their heads! They jumped apart as soon as the frame hit the wall. A piece of glass shot out and cut Rance on the cheek. The two of them stared at the mantle trying to make sense of what happened.

Before my mom could even offer to get him a bandage for his cheek, Rance told her he had to go and ran out the door. What a hero, huh? Suppose I was some kind of crazy killer poltergeist!

My dad would have stayed.

September 1, 2001
Dear Diary,
Mom found another guy. She met him at the gym the day after Rance dumped her, and she's been with him constantly ever since. He came over to the house yesterday, although my mom was obviously worried something strange would happen while he was there. She was right to worry because I tried my hardest to throw some stuff around, but this time, my hands passed through everything like they usually do. Mom couldn't hear me no matter how loudly I shouted. I guess I can only affect the physical world if I get super mad, and the two of them didn't do anything that got me really angry.

This guy isn't as handsome as Rance and he seems a lot nicer, but I still hate him. Hopefully, the next time he comes over and tries to make a move on her, I'll be able to throw an ashtray at his head.

September 11, 2001
Dear Diary,
It started in the early morning. Mom spent the night at her new boyfriend's place, so she wasn't here when the phone began to ring. The machine picked it up and I heard my Aunt Shelley's voice through the tinny speaker.

"Kimberly?" she asked. "Are you there? Have you seen what happened? Do you know if Joe is all right? Call me as soon as you can."

A few minutes passed and the phone rang again. This time it was Ken, Joe's best friend from high school. Then my Uncle Chris called, and my cousin, Dave, and my mom's best friend, Carmen—they all asked the same question: "Do you know if Joe is all right?" The phone kept ringing until there was no more room in the machine's memory to hold all the messages. The last one came from Nicole's mother, who called to say she had been trying to get a hold of her daughter, but all she kept getting was their answering machine.

Not long after she called, my dad burst through the front door. His suit was disheveled and his face was pale, except for his eyes, which were red from crying. He called out for my mother, but she wasn't there. He saw the flashing red light on the answering machine and listened to all the messages, then he just stood there for a very long time. Finally, after what seemed like forever, he picked up the remote control and turned on the TV.

It was like a scene from a movie, but it was playing on every channel with people screaming and crying, knowing that they had just witnessed the worst event of their entire lives. There was so much smoke and fire! It seemed like the beginning of the end of the world when the two towers fell.

My dad couldn't take it— he ran to the bathroom and threw up. He was still in there when my mom came home. They hugged each other. No, hug isn't the right word. They grabbed each other as if they were standing on the edge of a cliff and a strong wind was about to blow them over. My mom looked over his shoulder, saw the flashing red light and asked if there was a message from Joe. Dad just shook his head and she began to cry. She would have fallen to the floor if my dad hadn't been holding her up.

The phone rang again. Mom leapt out of my dad's arms and answered it. It was Nicole's mom again. The two of them talked for a long time and tried to calm each other, but it didn't work. They promised to call each other as soon as they heard anything. Mom then tried to call Nicole. The phone rang and rang, but no one answered. As the hours passed—more slowly than I ever thought possible—everyone who had ever cared about Joe called to ask if they knew if he was okay.

My mom was the one who talked to all of them. My dad just sat silently on the couch. He was still wearing his tie and jacket and the color wouldn't return to his face. He tried a few times to turn on the TV, but every time he did he saw the same images and had to turn it off.

There was no way they could ever have dreamed this would happen. Joe was dead. Their only other child was gone. All they could do was sit and wait until the moment their fears were confirmed and their grief could begin.

I didn't join them in their daze because I refused to even consider the possibility that he was gone. If he was, then why wasn't he here with me? The first thing I did when I died was find my family. I knew that Joe would do the same thing and since he wasn't there with us—with me—maybe there was a chance he was still alive.

I clung to this belief until around 3:00 PM when the phone rang and mom picked it up and heard Nicole's quivering voice on the other end. She spoke in between sobs, and it took her a long time to explain what had happened. My mom just listened.

Nicole had been sick and stayed home the past couple of days. She had been coughing in bed last night until she took some medicine, the kind that knocked her out. When Joe got up to leave for work, she was still asleep and—so she wouldn't be disturbed—he turned off their phone. So she heard nothing when people started calling her. She slept until half past two and, feeling better, she sat up in bed and turned on their TV. She changed the channel; it was there again and again and again. She ran to their phone and saw the red light beeping faster than it ever had before. The first message caused her to collapse onto the floor.

It was from Joe.

She played it for us.

"Nicole," he said, his voice filled with panic and confusion, "something's happened. They've told us to evacuate. I'm heading down the stairs right now. I know you're asleep and you couldn't hear the phone ring because I turned it off, but I wanted to let you know—in case anything happens to me—that I love you and know without a doubt that you are the strongest person I have ever met. No matter what happens, you will get through it. I will always love you and if I get out of here, I will love you even more than I ever thought I could.

I—" He paused and there was lots of background noise. "I—have to call my parents." he finally managed. He began to speak once more before his phone went dead and the message ended.

The waiting was over. We all knew for sure. My mom dropped the phone and fell to the floor and started to cry. My dad fell down beside her and held her. Nicole was crying and hung up.

I didn't cry. I wouldn't have if I could. I was too angry. Joe was dead, but he wasn't here. He didn't come to us. The one person who could help me fight the loneliness and understand the pain as I watched Mom and Dad self-destruct before my non-existent phantom eyes, and he stood me up to go wherever he decided to go. I felt so mad the only way to let the feeling go was to beat the crap out of it.

I did it in one punch.

I felt my spirit tingle like it had that night Rance came over. I felt it shake and vibrate, like it was a real physical thing and not just a floating collection of memories and thoughts. I felt my fist as it flew toward the wall in front of me. I felt it as it burst through the plaster and drywall and wood. I felt the pain surge through my arm, and I realized that this was the first time—including when I was alive—that I had ever felt something so much, and as soon as I did the feeling was gone and I wasn't angry anymore.

Most people would be disturbed to see a hole suddenly appear in the wall in front of them, but my parents didn't even flinch.

"What was that?" was the best response my dad could muster.

My mom looked up and saw the hole and answered him through her tears. "It was Samantha," she explained.

He looked back at the hole and thought about it for a few seconds. "Oh," he finally answered her. "Yeah. Of course it was."

September 18, 2001
Dear Diary,
My dad has officially moved back into the house. He's been living here the past week. Everyone at his office knew what happened to Joe, and his boss called to tell him they didn't expect him to come in until he feels ready. My mom refused to leave the house. They spent most of the time just lying in bed together. No one else could possibly understand. Two children gone within one year. None of their other problems seemed to matter anymore. Lying there, they forgot every hurtful thing they ever said to each other.

The phone would ring and they wouldn't answer it. The local news tried to interview them, but they refused. Their grief was their own. The only person they talked to was Nicole, who was going through the exact same thing they were. They didn't say much on the phone. Often minutes would often pass in silence, but they needed the connection with Nicole.

I still haven't heard from Joe. I thought maybe his absence had something to do with how far away he was. I only had to travel down a hospital hallway to get to my family, but he was over a thousand miles away and I didn't know how long it takes a spirit to go that far. Maybe he decided to stay with Nicole. I hope that's what he did, because I hate to think that he would be anywhere else.

September 30, 2001

Dear Diary,

Dad went back to work and Mom finally started to leave the house. Both of them are still very fragile, but they are on their way to mending. After all that happened, they forgot about the lawsuit they filed against the hospital where I died. It turned out that the hospital decided to avoid going to court and offered a $250,000 settlement, which they accepted. Dad made some comments about investing the money, but after one look from my mom, he decided that it probably wasn't the best idea.

October 13, 2001

Dear Diary,

I just looked over all the things I've written since I started this journal and I'm shocked by how much I've changed over the year. When I was alive, I never questioned or even really thought about what was going on around me. But now, as a ghost, observing is the only thing I can do. I would have to be the world's biggest idiot not to have this experience change the way I think.

And now, after a year spent thinking mostly about other people, I can't even remember why I was so angry at Jenny or why I was so crazy about Aidan.

October 27, 2001

Dear Diary,

Some days I just like to spend time in my old room. Neither of my parents has even stepped into it during the past year, so it's a good place to get away and be alone. I was in there today, looking at the photographs on my walls, when

I saw a piece of paper on my bed. It hadn't been there before, so I went to see what it was. It was a short note written in familiar handwriting.

Hey Kiddo,
What are you doing down there? I've been waiting for you for more than a month now. I figured you'd be here to greet me when I arrived, but no, I was told that you insisted on lingering on to the real world. What's up with that? You're dead! Get over it! Stop being a baby and get your butt over here where you belong. C'mon, it's really cool here and not at all like I pictured it. Don't be one of those spirits they write cheesy books about!

Love,
Joe

I had to read it a hundred times before I believed it really existed, and then I had to read it a hundred more before I could decide what to do next.

I'm going to see Joe. It's time. I've been here long enough.

I can't wait to talk to him. I feel like he's going to be meeting me for the very first time. I think he'll be surprised by how much his little sister has changed in the year after she died!

It may be a while before I can write to you again, Diary, but I promise to let you know what's going on as soon as I possibly can.

I hope I have good news!

Reality Television

"So what do you think?" Lorraine asked as she and her associates walked through the long main hallway of the dilapidated building.

"This could work," answered her partner, Darren, "it definitely feels haunted."

"Doesn't it? And the great thing is that this place used to be an insane asylum. Isn't that perfect?"

"I dunno," mumbled Jamie, the director. "Isn't that a bit too cliché?"

"This is TV," Lorraine reminded him. "There's no such thing as 'too cliché.' "

Together, the three of them made an odd sight inside the condemned structure. Lorraine and Darren's production company, Symbolton Productions, was the leading producer of programming for the fledging Real Life Network (RLN), a new channel devoted solely to "reality" TV shows. The name of the network and the genre they worked in never failed to amuse them, as they were fully aware that the last thing they would ever show in one of their productions was something that could be confused with "real life" or "reality." They had had their biggest success with a show called "And The Strongest Will Survive," which consisted of stranding 12 strangers in the middle of Death Valley during the summer and torturing them with countless annoyances until the contestants demanded to leave. The last one to beg to be taken home was named the winner and given $250,000 and a trip to Alaska.

They were touring through the damaged remains of the building because they had just received the go-ahead to film a new pilot based on their latest pitch. The working title was "'Til the Break of Dawn" and the concept was fairly simple: a group of four people—two men and two women—would have to the spend the night in a "haunted" building and whoever managed to stay inside it until sunrise would share in the $100,000 grand prize. The catch—every show needed a catch—was that only the most skeptical people who applied to be contestants were accepted. People who admitted to the producers that they actually believed in ghosts were immediately cut from the list. Lorraine and Darren figured that if they created a frightening enough environment, then even the most incredulous contestants were bound to let their imagination run wild and lose it on camera. This, they felt, would be more satisfying and entertaining than watching people who were already afraid to begin with.

"Taking cocky people down a peg," was how Darren pitched it to the executives at the network. "There's nothing our audience likes to see more than smart, well-educated people making total jackasses of themselves."

Filming of the pilot episode was to begin in three weeks, and they wanted to find just the right place to start things off. That was why they were walking inside the old Cravenhearst Sanitarium, which was located about six hours away from Los Angeles in the deserted town of Milton's Paradise, California. From the outside, the large building looked like a modern castle after a devastating siege from an unstoppable barbarian horde. Whole chunks of stone were missing from its outer walls, and it looked as though merely walking by them too fast could topple over the pillars that stood in front of the entrance. Vines crawled over everything and ominous wrought iron bars covered the windows, whose glass panes had been shattered long ago. Inside it was even better. The floors were covered with water and the walls were covered with graffiti. Paper and garbage mingled with broken furniture and shards of glass. Thanks to the efforts of hundreds of trespassers and vandals throughout the years, everything inside the building that could have been destroyed had been.

"So? Is this the place?" asked Lorraine.

Everyone nodded. The place was perfect.

* * *

Kyla, Symbolton's casting director, had been around long enough to know that when Lorraine and Darren asked for "normal, average-looking contestants" that they meant average and normal for television. So she searched for a quartet of fit, attractive 20-somethings who were bright and skeptical enough to find the whole concept of the show ridiculous. Men and women of that description sat and waited for hours outside her office as she interviewed them one by one to find the perfect four for the first show.

Patient almost to the point of sainthood, she took a sip from her coffee and told her assistant to bring in the next candidate. When he walked in, she wasn't impressed. He was tall, handsome and athletic, but that description fit most of the men she had seen (and quite a few of the women as well) so she wasn't expecting much when she began the interview. She looked at the completed questionnaire he had handed to her as he sat down in the chair in front of her desk.

"So," she said, scanning the paper for his name. "Brad. What do you know about this show we're putting together?"

Brad shrugged.

"Absolutely nothing," he admitted with a smile. "I'm just here because my girlfriend wanted me to come with her and I couldn't think of a way to get out of it."

Kyla appreciated his honesty and the fact that he didn't appear to be overeager. A reluctant contestant was more interesting than someone who would do anything just to be on television.

"Well, what we're doing is sending a group of four strangers into a haunted insane asylum and whoever remains in the building by sunrise gets to split the $100,000 prize."

"Oh," Brad replied, "so you're looking for nervous, crazy types then?"

Kyla laughed. "Not exactly. Do you believe in ghosts or anything at all supernatural?"

"Does Michael Jackson count? That guy's been spooky for over a decade now."

"No." She shook her head with an amused grin.

"Well, then no I don't," he admitted. "I think whenever someone talks about seeing a ghost, they're really saying 'I have an overactive imagination' or—more likely— 'the prescription for my crazy pills just ran out.' I suppose that would be a problem, huh?"

"I didn't say that," she answered. "Now it says here that you're getting your Masters in English literature?"

"Yes, I've got itchins for Dickens."

"You don't look like an English grad."

He pulled out a pair of glasses and put them on. He then mussed up his hair and pulled a paperback copy of James Joyce's *Ulysses* out of his back pocket. "How about now?" he asked.

She laughed and wrote *A definite maybe* on his form before she told him he could go.

By the end of the week, she had managed to find 20 suitable candidates for the show and she presented them to the producers, who put them all through another interview. Darren and Lorraine were especially impressed by a young woman named Lynne, who was an elementary school teacher by day and a part-time bartender by night. They loved her wit and candor and how she looked in the t-shirt and jeans she had been wearing. They also loved Brad as much as Kyla had, along with a goofy, young actor named John and a not-particularly bright, but spectacularly gorgeous, young fitness model named Veronica.

"This is our foursome," Lorraine decided. "They're just sexy and smart enough that people will root both for them and against them."

"Definitely," Darren agreed. "That Brad guy is perfect. He's attractive *and* a know-it-all smartass. People are going to love him and hate him."

With the producer's blessing, Kyla phoned the four approved contenders and told them that they had been cast and that they would all be filming in a week's time. Their reactions were mixed. Veronica screamed aloud when she was told she would be appearing on the show, and Kyla could tell that she was also jumping up and down. Lynne was much more reserved and simply thanked Kyla for the opportunity to try something interesting. John's reaction was the most muted, as he wasn't sure how he felt about his first successful audition. Brad sounded amused by the whole thing, and when Kyla asked him if thought he'd end up taking some money home, he just laughed and said, "I've already spent it."

Seven days later, the four contestants were introduced to each other in front of the minivan that was transporting them from L.A. to Milton's Paradise. It took exactly five minutes for them to establish their roles on the show. Lynne was the tough no-nonsense leader who valued common sense and practicality over all things. John was the wiseass who never failed to find a punch line when given a set-up. Veronica was the naive innocent, the one most unlikely to last the whole night and Brad was the quiet one.

Brad had every reason to stay silent as he sat in the backseat of the van and smiled as John made another lame joke. He had totally scammed Kyla and the producers when he told them that he was just there because of his girlfriend. He didn't have a girlfriend, and not only had he known what the show was about when he auditioned for it, he also—thanks to a friend who worked as an intern at Symbolton—knew they were looking for skeptics. He also knew that everything on the show—no matter how disturbing it was—was going to be faked. Knowing this, he planned to play the voice of reason through most of the night. He would dismiss almost everything that happened to them as the hours went by, but then—slowly—he would start to lose his cool, which would help unnerve the other contestants and—hopefully—convince them that the place *was* really haunted and their lives would be best served by getting out as soon as their feet could carry them. He would then be the only person left and the only one to pocket the $100,000.

What he hadn't counted on was the fact that Lynne also had a friend who worked at Symbolton and that she was operating on the exact same game plan. Neither of them knew it, but the best they could hope for—given their

certainty that the show was fixed—was convincing Veronica and John to leave and then splitting the prize.

John was leafing through the folder a production assistant had handed to them when they arrived at the studio. It contained a map of the asylum, the waiver they had to sign before filming could begin and a brief history of Dr. Hugo Cravenhearst, the man who had founded the sanitarium that bore his name.

"They have to have made this guy up!" He laughed as he read the bio. "None of this can be true. It says here he used to use a hammer and spike to create holes in people's skulls so the demons who were possessing their minds could be freed."

"It's true!" Lynne and Brad answered him the same time.

"I looked him up on the Internet," Lynne added.

"I went to the library and found a couple of books about him," Brad one-upped her. "Everything this bio says is true, really did happen. This Cravenhearst guy was far nuttier than anyone who was ever sent to be treated by him."

"How did he get away with it?" asked Veronica. "If he was so crazy, why didn't anyone stop him?"

"They did," answered Lynne. "It just took them awhile. Finally his abuses became so intolerable that his patients revolted against him and his staff. They were so enraged they literally tore him and the others apart, and then they turned on each other. Almost no one survived the night and those who did never ever talked about it. After that, the place was closed and no one has been in there since."

"Except for the show's producers, crew and about a thousand different vandals," Brad added.

"Yeah, except them." Lynne frowned. She didn't like to be corrected.

"Wow," John remarked, "maybe this place really is haunted."

"Do you really think so?" asked Veronica.

Both Lynne and Brad laughed. "No," they both insisted, each annoyed that the other responded alike.

* * *

Jamie was edging close toward a breakdown.

"Why can't I see anything from camera 13?" he screamed into his headset. "Damn it, people! We start shooting in three hours and all the cameras aren't working? Do I have to fix it myself!" he shouted, cursing Lorraine and Darren's decision to try something innovative.

He would have been happy just to follow the contestants with a couple of handheld cameras, but the producers felt that the presence of the cameramen would be too much of a distraction. Their solution was to outfit the contestants with headsets that had cameras built into them, and to place regular remote-controlled cameras throughout the building. That made his job 10 times more complicated than it should have been and he wasn't happy about it.

While he shouted out commands in the large trailer that sat outside the building, Lorraine and Darren were talking to the actor they had hired to host the show in an equally large motor home. Chip Detmer was a hip, young comedian whose sitcom had just been cancelled, but whose face was recognizable enough to pull in viewers. A prankster at heart, he loved the show's premise and seemed genuinely excited to be involved. He especially loved the idea of the stunt that they planned to open the show with.

"Okay, just so I know we're on the same page here. I walk into the room, introduce myself and tell them the rules and a little bit about the history of the place, and just when I say that it's time to start, some maniac is going to come up from behind me and stab me in front of them?"

"That's it," Darren confirmed.

"That's great," Chip cackled. "They are going to be *freaked!*"

* * *

The contestants' minivan drove up to the sanitarium two hours before filming was to begin. Even though the lighting and type of cameras involved made it unnecessary, they all spent an hour in hair and makeup, coming out looking almost no different than when they came in. All four of them were then outfitted with their microphones and their camera headsets, which ran on two surprisingly heavy batteries that sat in the backpacks they were given. The backpacks all contained flashlights, water and some food. That was all they were given to make it through the night, but they didn't seem overly concerned, Brad especially.

"It's not like we're camping," he explained when Veronica expressed surprise by how little they were given. "All we have to do is pretend to be scared while walking through an old building for 10 hours. You don't need a lot of supplies for that."

When they were all set up, one of Jamie's assistants led them into the sanitarium and into a large room that had once been a dormitory. It was dimly lit by a few of the lights that had been brought in by the crew. She told them the show would begin when they saw Chip.

The room was dank and smelled of mildew and urine.

"This is *so* gross," said Veronica, but the inflection of her voice indicated an almost giddy awe rather than a sense of disgust. She was getting into this situation and was ready to have some fun.

"Yeah," Brad said, "somehow I think it's going to get much worse."

"As long as they don't do anything with rats," John said grimacing. "I can't handle rats."

"Are there any other phobias we should look out for?" asked Brad.

"I hate moths," answered Lynne.

"I'm not good with dogs," admitted Veronica.

"Okay, rats, dogs and moths are to be avoided at all costs."

"What about you?" asked John.

Brad thought about this for a second. "My ex-girlfriend," he said, "but even she wouldn't come all the way out here just to scare me. I hope."

None of them had been allowed to take watches or any other kind of timepiece with them, so they had no idea how long they would have to wait until Chip arrived. Sensing it would be a good time to do some mental work on the other contestants, both Lynne and Brad started to speak. Brad managed to beat Lynne to the punch.

"So," he mused, "what do you think they're going to throw at us?"

"What do you mean?" asked Veronica.

"What kind of tricks are they going to pull on us? I mean, think about it, even if this place *was* haunted—and that's a big if—there would be no way for them to predict how the so-called spooks appeared in front of us. Hell, this place could be loaded knee-deep with ghosts and that would still be no guarantee that any one of them would feel the need to scare the crap out of us—"

"Brad's right," Lynne interrupted him, as she also wanted to be the voice of reason. "The only way they're going to get the show they want is by faking everything we see and hear."

"Do you really think so?" asked Veronica, who—unbeknownst to the others—wasn't nearly as innocent as she appeared. She was actually as cynical as Brad and Lynne, but hoped that she might have an advantage if they dismissed her as just another pretty blonde airhead. Ironically, John—the actor—was the only person not playing a role that night. Still, he responded to what Brad and Lynne said with a shrug.

"Yeah, but so what?" he responded. "I don't care if it's fake or not, scary is scary and once something like fear takes a hold of you, it doesn't matter how real it is or not. Like I said before, I'm scared of rats and you don't have to fake a rat. They could have a room that's full of them and if there is, then I'm out of here."

* * *

At that moment, in the trailer outside the asylum, Darren and Lorraine—who could hear everything the four contestants were saying over their microphones—both cursed themselves for not stuffing one of the hospital's room's full of rats.

"It would have been great," Darren said.

"Yeah," Lorraine agreed, "but then we'd have to deal with the animal rights people and make sure none of the rats got hurt..."

"Right," Darren said, "if one of those guys stomped on one of the little rodents, we'd have PETA up our butts so fast."

"What we have is fine, right?" Lorraine wondered.

"It would scare me," said Darren, "and I've seen you with your makeup off, so I know the true meaning of fear."

She tried not to laugh as she punched him playfully in the arm.

"Five minutes to air," Jamie's assistant Daphne informed the crew over their headsets.

"This is it. Are you excited?"

"As I'll ever be," Lorraine replied.

* * *

The four contestants were sitting quietly in the dormitory when the door opened and a short but muscular young man walked in and joined them.

"Hi guys, I'm your host, Chip Detmer, and I want to welcome you to the first episode of 'Til the Break of Dawn.' Are you excited?"

They all nodded.

"That's great. Now I'm here to tell you about the rules of our game and a little about where you are. The rules are simple. All you guys have to do is stay inside this building until sunrise, which is going to happen 10 hours from now. That's it. If all of you do it then you get to split the $100,000 grand prize, but there is a catch." Chip paused to let the drama build. "This building is the infamous Cravenhearst Sanitarium and it will require a lot more than just your average, everyday bravery to stay inside."

Brad smirked at this but managed to stay quiet.

"If you leave the building before sunrise, then you forfeit your share of the prize money. Now that you know that, let me tell you a little about where you are. Cravenhearst was founded 125 years ago by Dr. Hugo Cravenhearst, a well-known reverend who had some very unique ideas about mental illness. He believed that insanity was the result of a person being possessed by evil spirits, and here in this building, he tried to cure his patients by beating and shocking the evil out of them. Of course, many of them died before they could be cured. The building had only been operational for 23 years when the sanitarium was permanently shut down, but in that time, it is believed that as many as 400 people died within its walls. I ask you to please be careful so that by tomorrow that number isn't 404—"

At that moment thunder roared from outside and the lights inside the dormitory went out, plunging the room into complete darkness. All four of the contestants scrambled to get their flashlights from out of their backpacks. They turned them on and shone them at Chip, who was in the same spot as he had been before.

Chip smiled and continued. "I think someone or some*thing* knows you're here. Now remember, you've got to stay in here until sunrise to claim the money. Leave even a—"

It was Veronica who first caught sight of a 'some*thing*' approaching Chip from behind. Purely out of reflex she screamed and he turned toward it. It was something that appeared to be human, but just barely. Its face was long and gaunt, and its mouth seemingly caught in the grip of a permanent silent scream. It had no eyes—just black holes as dark as forever as it approached. It was dressed in a white hospital gown and it carried a large hypodermic needle in its right hand. Chip screamed and the creature raised up the needle and drove it into his chest as hard as it could. Chip fell to the ground as blood gushed out of a severed artery. The creature stabbed him four more times before it stopped and turned its attention to the four people watching with shocked expressions on their faces.

Knowing that the show had started, they took this as their cue and ran screaming past their host and his murderer into the sanitarium.

"And so it begins," Brad whispered to himself as he ran through the door.

"That was *so* cool," Veronica added as she followed behind him.

* * *

Darren looked over to Lorraine to see if she looked as confused as he was. She turned to him and whispered under her breath so Jamie and his assistant couldn't hear her.

"Did you recast the guy who was supposed to kill Chip?" she asked.

He turned to face her, but he couldn't speak. It was evident in his eyes that he hadn't. He shook his head and she began to panic.

"Who the hell was that?"

"I don't know," answered Darren. "I never saw that guy before in my life. Did you see the makeup on him? We couldn't afford something as sophisticated as that."

Jamie overheard them and turned toward them from his chair in front of the wall of monitors.

"What are you two yammering about?" he asked, annoyed by their nervous chatter. He was surprised by how pale they both looked. "What's going on?"

Darren's voice was weak. "Jamie, could you pull up the camera in the dormitory?"

"Why? They just left there and they're heading in the opposite direction."

"Please, Jamie," Lorraine insisted.

Jamie shrugged. "Give me camera Number 2," he ordered Daphne.

Like all of the cameras, Number 2 was equipped with a night vision capability that captured what it saw in a eerie green glow.

"What is that?" Jamie asked when he noticed something on the ground. "Is that Chip? What is he still doing on the floor?" He flipped a switch that allowed him to give directions to Chip through the receiver the young actor wore in his ear. "Chip?" he spoke into his mike. "They're gone. You can get out of there now."

As they focused on the still body lying on the floor, Daphne noticed something moving in the corner of the room and pointed to it.

"What's that?'

"Turn on the lights," ordered Lorraine.

Daphne nodded and flipped another switch. The lights went back on in the dormitory. Chip was on the ground, his body soaking in a pool of dark, thick red liquid.

"Is that real blood?" asked Jamie, before the thing in the corner rushed toward the room's camera. It moved so fast none of them got a good look at it. They saw only a hand that looked more like a claw and a mouth that was filled with far too many teeth. It hit the camera and the monitor was instantly overtaken by static.

"What the—" Jamie swore as the other three jumped and covered their eyes.

"*What was that?*" Lorraine couldn't keep herself from screaming.

Jamie barked orders to the crew inside the building through his headset. "Mandy, Fred, get your butt into the dormitory! Something's happened to Chip."

There was no response.

"Mandy? Fred?" he asked again. "Joe? Glenn? Beck? Can any of you hear me?"

No one responded.

"Daphne, turn on all the cameras in the rooms that the crew members are supposed to be in."

Her hands shaking, Daphne did like he asked and each monitor in front of them became filled with static.

"There's nothing," She said, her voice breaking. "All of the cameras in those rooms are gone."

She checked all of the cameras and found that the only ones that were still working were the ones being worn by Brad, Lynne, John and Veronica.

Jamie turned to the producers, suspecting they might have something to do with this. "What's going on?"

Darren tried to speak. "That thing that attacked Chip...we never saw it before...it was...it was *real*."

Daphne attempted to get in touch with someone—anyone—from the crew who was inside the building. She got no response at all.

"They're gone," she whispered disbelievingly. "All of them are gone."

* * *

So far the four contestants were somewhat underwhelmed by what they had come across. The place was dark and musty and full of garbage, but it wasn't that scary. They had spent the last 10 minutes walking down a corridor, most of whose rooms were sealed shut because of limited camera availability.

"Hel-lo," Brad shouted playfully, "I'm not feeling the terror, folks!"

Veronica smiled. "I don't know, that murder was pretty scary."

Brad rolled his eyes. "Please, that was *so* fake. You'd figure they'd have a big enough budget to get real-looking blood."

"Looked pretty real to me," John admitted.

"I've got to agree with Brad on this one," said Lynne. "They're going to have to do a lot better than that if they're going to get me to give up my share of the cash."

Brad turned and aimed his flashlight at an open door at the end of the hallway.

"Well, look what we've got here. An open doorway. Do you think that we'll regret it if we walk through it?"

"Absolutely," John replied and grinned.

"Biggest mistake of our lives," Lynne deadpanned.

"I hope they have something good in there," said Veronica.

* * *

Darren and Lorraine returned breathlessly back to the trailer.

"The doors are sealed shut," Darren informed Jamie and Daphne. "We couldn't get inside the sanitarium."

"And," Lorraine joined in, "our cell phones won't work and our cars won't start. We're alone out here."

"It could be worse," Jamie muttered as he watched the four contestants walk into a room that was supposed to have been locked up and made off limits. "We could be alone *in there*."

* * *

"This must have been where they gave the crazies their shock treatments," John guessed, basing his theory on the large, threatening machine in the room's right-hand corner. Wires connected the machine to the table in the middle of the room, which had a heavy brown leather strap on each of its corners that had obviously been used to help restrain whoever had been unlucky enough to have been forced to lay on it.

"This place looks medieval," remarked Lynne.

"I bet it was even scarier when it was operational," said Brad.

"How do you think it worked?" asked Veronica.

Lynne examined the table and the contraption and figured it out. "It's pretty simple," she said. "They strapped you onto here and placed these electrodes to your temples and wherever else they thought it was important, and then they flipped the switch over there," she pointed to the machine, "and then the patient would get a head full of lightning."

"That," John surmised, "would suck."

Brad spotted something. "There's a sign here," he told everyone. He used his flashlight to read it. "'It is only in the presence of His Grace that we can find peace.'"

"That doesn't sound so evil," said Veronica.

"It does if you realize that it's referring to that," John pointed to the machine in the corner. He walked over to it. "See," he showed them. Engraved on the box were the words "His Grace." "I wonder if this thing still works," he said as he flipped one of its switches.

All at once the room lit up like a fireworks display and a scream of pain and horror echoed through their ears. There in the middle of the room they saw the ghostly apparition of a young woman strapped onto the table. The electricity surged through her and caused her to emit an almost fluorescent glow.

"Switch it off!" shouted Lynne.

John turned the machine off and the woman vanished instantly. The room was dark once again, and the four contestants all struggled to keep their composure.

"That," remarked Brad, "was amazing. I didn't even know you could do that. Try it again," he said to John. "See if it still works."

John flipped the switch again, but this time nothing happened.

"How did they do that?" he asked, amazed by the spectacle he had just seen.

No one answered him.

* * *

The four people in the trailer could not believe what they had just seen.

"Was that one of ours?" asked Lorraine, even though she knew the answer.

"Are you kidding?" answered Darren. "Do you know how much something like that would have cost?"

"What are they still doing in there?" asked Daphne. "Why aren't they running away?"

"Because," Jamie sighed, "they think we faked it."

"How could we do something like that?"

"We couldn't, but they don't know that."

"What are they doing now?" asked Lorraine, who couldn't even look at the screen anymore.

"They're walking back into the hallway."

* * *

The foursome had split up to explore the rooms of another corridor.

"Hey guys!" Lynne shouted to the others. "I found a stairway."

"Up or down?" Brad yelled back.

"Down."

"The basement?" said John, "that can't be good."

"Want to go down?" asked Lynne.

The three of them answered her by running toward her.

Veronica couldn't help but giggle. "They've got to have something really good down there."

Lynne was the first one down the long, dark staircase. Her flashlight was barely strong enough to break the darkness in front of her. Upstairs, the broken windows allowed for some moonlight to shine in, but down there was only pitch-black darkness.

"Did I say I was frightened of my ex-girlfriend?" asked Brad. "Because I meant to say that I'm scared of the dark."

"Did you hear that?" asked Lynne as she approached the bottom steps.

"No. What is it?" asked Veronica.

"Like little footsteps. Lots of them. And squeaking noises."

John turned pale. "Please, don't let it be rats," he prayed to no one in particular.

Lynne reached the basement floor and shined her flashlight on the ground. "I don't see any."

They flashed their lights around and found no evidence of any kind of rodent, but they could still hear something moving around.

John sighed with relief. "It's a tape recording," he told everybody, "and a cheesy one at that."

Emboldened by this realization he stepped away from the group and moved further down the basement. He was about 20 feet away from them when he began to scream. His flashlight dropped to the ground as he used his hands to swat at his body. He was covered with over a hundred different rats. The other three ran to him and shone their flashlights on him. Veronica screamed and began to panic while Brad and Lynne fought to remain calm and tried to help John get them off his body. Brad bravely reached out for one, but his hand passed right through it. The same thing happened to Lynne.

"Get them off me!" screamed John. "I can feel them! They're all over me!"

Brad and Lynne tried to help him, but nothing they could do seemed to work. Lynne stopped for a moment to think of something else they could try, when she heard the sound of a thousand fluttering wings. She turned and screamed when her flashlight caught sight of the swarm of moths that was headed directly for her. They surrounded her and she dropped her flashlight as she tried to swat them away.

Both Brad and Veronica were overwhelmed with what was happening. Brad tried to run back and forth between John and Lynne while they screamed and struggled, but there was nothing he could do for either of them. Veronica was unable to move. From behind her she heard the unmistakable sound of a cruel and hungry growl. She began to cry as she turned around. The beast's eyes were blood red and its yellowing teeth were covered with dripping blood and saliva. As it lunged for her she screamed and dropped her flashlight, leaving Brad with the only source of light. Even more helpless than before, he tried to help Veronica as she struggled with the demon dog, but as he fought with the animal, his flashlight began to flicker.

"Don't do this to me," he yelled at it. "I can't take the dark!"

As if on cue his flashlight's light bulb faded and left the four of them screaming and struggling in total darkness.

* * *

Thanks to the cameras' night vision feature, everyone in the trailer could see that the four contestants were struggling with a variety of invisible menaces. John was jumping up and down and grabbing at his body, while Lynne was covering her eyes as she swatted frantically into the air. Veronica was on her back and looked like she was barely holding off something larger, and Brad was just cowering on the floor with his hands in front of his eyes.

"What's happening to them?" asked Daphne.

No one had an answer for her.

"Didn't we set up some lights down there? For the crew to work with," Darren remembered.

"You're right," Jamie answered him as he tried to find the button that could turn them on. "There." He found it.

* * *

The basement filled up with light and Lynne, Veronica and John all fell to the floor from exhaustion. Their nightmares had vanished as soon as the light appeared and they struggled to regain their breath as they lay flat on their backs. Brad removed his hands from his eyes and was the first person to really see what the basement looked like. It was fashioned out of wood and concrete and was full of a variety of different props. He got up and grabbed one of them. It was a large blood-covered hypodermic needle, identical to the one used on Chip.

"These guys are brilliant." His voice was full of respectful awe.

"What are you talking about?" John asked as he gulped for air.

"They know we're going to dismiss everything they do as fake," Brad explained, "so they get us down here, freak us out and then turn the lights on and show us all their props. They want us to think that they couldn't pull off something so sophisticated when all they have is junk like this." He lifted up another prop, a skull-shaped mask, to prove his point.

"Let me get this straight." Lynne was finally starting to calm down. "You think they just faked that?"

"Yeah."

"How?"

"I don't know. Holograms, 3-D projection, whatever. They're from Hollywood, this is what they do."

"But we all felt them," Veronica insisted.

"Did you? Or did it seem so real, you thought you felt it? When Lynne and I tried to get those rats off of John, our hands passed right through them like they weren't there. The mind can play funny tricks on people. You guys were so scared by what you saw, your minds told you that they were really there, when they weren't. It's pure Psych 101."

"I don't know," said John, unconvinced.

"Well, if you guys think what just happened was real, then go ahead and leave right now. It'll just mean more money for me," Brad said.

Lynne stood up. "That's not going to happen," she told him.

Veronica and John followed her up.

"I can't wait to see how they're going to top that," remarked Veronica.

"If I see just one more rat," John declared, "I'm out of here."

* * *

The four people in the trailer could not believe what they just seen and heard.

"They think we were behind *that!*" exclaimed Darren. "How stupid are they?"

Jamie thought about this. "Either they're really brave, they really need the money or they are the dumbest people who ever lived," he decided.

"Or all three," suggested Daphne.

"I'm beginning to think," Lorraine sighed, "that this show was flawed from its conception."

* * *

The four contestants decided to go back upstairs. They only had three working flashlights now, so Brad kept close to Veronica.

"You know," he said, "if they can do stuff like that, it makes you wonder what else they have in store for us."

"Maybe that was the best they had," suggested Veronica. "Maybe it's easy money from this point on."

The four of them turned a corner and found themselves at the edge of another staircase, but this one went up.

"Well, gang," Lynne asked everyone, "want to try this again?"

Cautiously, everyone began to walk up the stairs. Thanks to the moonlight, these stairs were not as dark as the basement stairs, but they represented a different challenge thanks to all the water and garbage that covered them. Both Veronica and John almost slipped going up. They moved closer to the edge and grasped firmly on the handrail, while Lynne managed to make it to the top without a problem. Brad was just about to meet her when he hit a wet patch and his foot slid out from under him. To the horror of the others he tumbled painfully down the stairs all the way to the floor, where he landed on his back.

He shouted up to them before they could follow him back down. "I'm okay," he told them, "it looked a lot worse than it felt."

He stood up and readjusted his helmet cam and did a quick injury check to make sure he hadn't broken anything. He hadn't, and was about to go back up the stairs, when Lynne noticed that a strange shape appeared to be following him.

"There's *something* behind you!" she shouted down to him.

Brad turned and his flashlight shone into the face of a very tall and lumbering *something*. It smelled of rotting meat and old formaldehyde and looked as though it had been put through a meat grinder at least three times and then haphazardly reassembled by someone who only had a vague recollection of what a human being was supposed to look like. Brad was almost struck dumb by the sight of the creature, then he realized it was just another crew member, like the guy who had "killed" Chip.

"Cool make-up, man," he congratulated the actor, who appeared to take his role too seriously to respond. Instead he grabbed Brad by the throat, lifted him off the ground and began to squeeze. Brad fought and kicked as hard as he could, but the lack of oxygen to his brain soon took all of the fight out of him.

"That thing's strangling him!" shouted John. "What do we do?"

There was a long agonizing moment as the three of them tried to figure out if Brad was actually in danger or if this was just another prank. The slackness of his body in the creature's hands convinced them to act quickly. The three of them ran down the stairs, but they all slipped on different wet patches and tumbled down. John was the first one to get to the floor and his body rammed squarely into the creature's legs. His impact was hard enough to cause the creature to drop Brad and topple over. Its body exploded into a hail of wet, meaty shrapnel as it hit the ground, covering the two men with chunks of reeking flesh.

Lynne and Veronica both landed on the floor. Lynne and John both managed to escape injury like Brad had, but Veronica had heard something snap during her way down. A bolt of pain rocketed through her left arm, and as she sat up, she realized that any attempt to move it caused even more pain.

John checked on how Brad was doing. His breathing was shallow, but he was still alive. He sat up and tried to speak, but the words would not pass through his windpipe. He pointed to John and started gesturing wildly.

"What is it?" John asked as he looked down to where Brad was pointing. He screamed when he saw the chunk of zombie meat on his shirt was moving. It appeared to be edging toward his throat before he reacted instinctively and swatted it off of his shirt. It landed on the floor and started moving again before he stomped on it until it was flat and completely still.

"Thiiiissssss isssssss re-allll," Brad hissed painfully, his words sticking in his throat.

Lynne was still dazed, but was aware enough to hear what Brad said.

"What did you say?" she asked him, her sides aching from the fall down the stairs.

"Re-allll," Brad repeated. "Thiiissss issssss re-allll!"

"Are you crazy?" she shouted.

He shook his head and lifted up another moving piece of the creature's scattered remains as proof of his statement.

John nodded in agreement.

"There's no way they could fake this," he insisted as he stomped on another piece of creeping zombie meat.

"You two are in this together," Lynne accused them.

"What are you talking about?" asked Veronica, her words tinged with pain.

"They're acting like this is the real deal so they can scare us out of here and out of our share of the money," she explained angrily.

"Don't you believe your own eyes?" John asked her incredulously.

"No! Not here! Not now!" she answered.

"Fine," he shrugged. "You can stay here and get killed. I'm leaving." He turned to Brad. "Are you coming?"

Brad lifted up his hand and felt the red mark that was burned around his neck. The pain was real. Whatever that thing was, it *had* tried to kill him, but doubts started to linger in his mind. He had *known* all of this stuff was going to be faked, he just hadn't expected that the producers would be so *good* at it. The doubts stopped lingering and took full control. Lynne was right. He couldn't trust his own eyes or any of his senses. He looked up at John and shook his head.

"No, I'm ssssstaying," he barely managed to say.

"You're crazy," John shook his head. "What about you?" he turned to Veronica. "We have to get you to a doctor or a hospital or something."

Veronica held her arm tightly to her body and shook her head. She was in a lot of pain, but nowhere near enough to get her to quit.

"I'm staying," she answered without hesitation.

John looked at her sadly before he turned away and started running alone down the corridor toward the nearest exit.

"Sucker," Lynne mocked him as she struggled to stand up.

"Real or not," Veronica decided, "when this thing is over I'm going to sue these guys for everything they've got."

* * *

"Did she say she was going to sue us?" asked Darren, who had stopped looking at the monitors a half an hour ago when he started to feel like he was going to have a nervous breakdown.

"Don't worry," answered Lorraine. "I'm pretty sure the waivers they signed absolve us of any injury caused by their participation in the show."

"Guys," Jamie interrupted them, "I've been thinking about something."

"What?" asked Lorraine.

"That thing—the one that looked like hamburger—"

"Yeah. What about it?" asked Darren.

"Didn't it look . . . I don't know . . . Fresh? Like it had just come out of the ground?" He didn't wait for them to answer him. "I know the people who ran this place were all freaks, but even they wouldn't bury people *inside* a sanitarium."

Daphne thought about this and turned pale.

"You don't think…?"

"It had to have come from outside the building," Jamie finished his thought.

Lorraine and Darren both jumped up.

"Are you saying—" Lorraine started to panic.

"—That there could be more of those things—" Darren interrupted.

"And they could be coming after—"

"Us?"

Before Jamie could answer them, Lorraine and Darren started grabbing everything they could find and piling it all in front of the trailer's door.

* * *

John ran to the first door he could find. It was locked. He slammed his body against it, but it was far too heavy for him to knock it down. He ran to another one but it too refused to open. All of the windows were barred, and it appeared that there was no exit in sight.

"How are we supposed to leave if you won't let us out?" he screamed out with frustration as he ran to find another way to escape.

Not knowing what else to do, he started running back to the door where they began, hoping that there might be another exit.

* * *

The other three contestants decided to try to make another attempt to climb up the stairs in front of them. Lynne, the only one not nursing a serious injury, made it up first and impatiently waited for the other two to join her. The pain had sapped away all of Veronica's sweetness, and she cursed aloud with each step she took. Brad had to fight against the dizzyness and nausea he felt as a reminder of his brain's recent struggle for oxygen and he could still barely speak above a raspy whisper.

When all three of them finally made it to the top of the stairs, they turned toward the hallway and saw nothing but doorways and darkness.

"This is stupid," Veronica muttered. "Why don't we just sit our asses down and wait until it's time to leave? There's no point in taking another risk by going forward."

"The contract," Brad rasped. "Didn't you read it?"

"No," she answered him truthfully.

"You should have." Lynne scowled. "It said very clearly that if we stay in any one spot for longer than half an hour we forfeit our share of money. Think about it. How exciting would the show be if we all just sat in one spot for 10 hours?"

"Those weasels think of everything," Veronica cursed as she followed the others into the dark hallway.

* * *

Even though the lights were on inside the dormitory, John still managed to trip over Chip's dead body. He fell forward, landing in the spot on the floor where Chip's blood had pooled. He jumped up as quickly as he could and began to scream when he saw the thick red liquid all over his hands and clothes. He looked down at Chip's corpse and knew once and for all that this was the real thing.

He ran to the door they had all entered from and found that it was now locked like all the others had been. He screamed out and threw himself against it. Unlike the other doors, John felt something give as he slammed into it and—thankfully—it wasn't his shoulder. He ran into it again and the door burst open, revealing a view of the dark moonlit outside world.

Refusing to waste even a second celebrating his escape, he ran out the door toward the light that came from the trailer in the distance. He felt like he was ready to collapse and was suddenly overcome with the paranoia that when he got inside the trailer, the producers would laugh at him for being so easily duped by their tricks.

But they didn't laugh at him. They weren't there. The trailer was empty. Its door had been ripped off its hinges and a pile of furniture and equipment littered the ground in front of it.

"Is anybody in here?" he called out when he walked inside it. All he got for a response was the sound of the other three contestants coming from a speaker. He turned and saw them walking down a dark hallway on three of the monitors in front of him. On the fourth he saw a series of images that looked like as though they were fading away into infinity and realized it was his camera capturing himself in the monitor. He took off his helmet and watched the others as they turned and walked into one of the rooms along the corridor. He looked at the console to see if there was anything he could do to help them, like turn on some lights or speak to them through some hidden speaker, but it was smashed beyond repair.

All he could do was watch.

They were in an office of some kind. At least it used to be an office. Now it was just a room filled with discarded paper and damaged furniture. Through the speaker he heard everything they said to each other.

"Nothing in here," Lynne concluded after they had looked through it.

"Good," said Veronica. "Nothing is good."

Brad stayed quiet and wandered over to the large desk that took up a fair amount of the room's space. He opened its top drawer and sighed and said something, but his voice was so quiet that John couldn't understand him.

Neither could Lynne.

"What did you say?" she asked him, shining her flashlight in his face.

Brad frowned and pointed into the drawer. Lynne walked over to him and shone her flashlight at what he was pointing to. She sighed as well.

"What is it?" asked Veronica.

"A skull," answered Lynne. "A human skull."

Veronica rolled her eyes. "They're not even trying anymore," she said as hugged her broken arm to her side.

Lynne reached in and lifted the skull out of the drawer.

"What are you doing?" asked Veronica. "Don't pick it up."

"Why not?" Lynne asked back. She looked at the skull and saw that it wasn't like the ones she had seen in museums or on television. It wasn't bleached white and it wasn't purely bone. Parts of it were still fleshy. "They did a good job on this one," she said. "It feels as real as it looks." She moved to set it down on the desk, but she stopped when she felt a weird sensation in her hands.

"What's wrong?" asked Veronica.

"I don't know," Lynne admitted. "It just felt like it was trying to move." She set it down on the desk and looked at it.

The skull sat there, as still and lifeless as any dead thing could be.

"I'm bored," said Veronica. "Let's keep moving. Walking keeps my mind off how much my arm hurts."

Lynne and Brad nodded and they turned to leave. The three of them started walking toward the door when a sound stopped them. It was a voice and it was coming from behind them.

"*The beginning is near*," the voice warned them. "*This place will be warm again.*"

They all turned around and saw that the voice was coming from the skull.

"*And when the fire comes you will know it*," it added.

"There's a speaker inside it," Lynne guessed, "and some gizmos to make its mouth move."

That sounded reasonable, so the three of them turned back and walked out of the room.

"Morons," John said, shaking his head disbelievingly. It then occurred to him that the same thing could be said about him. What the hell was he doing sticking around in the trailer when it was obvious that something horrible had happened to the people who had been inside of it? The smart thing to do would be to go out and find a car and "borrow" it so he could drive back to Los Angeles. He turned around and was about to leave when he was stopped by the sound of a horrible scream from the speakers. He turned back and could barely make out what was being captured on the TVs in front of him. Veronica, Lynne and Brad were all running as fast as they could, reducing their images on camera into a dark green blur. John stood there and watched as the three appeared to be pursued by an unseen assailant.

One of the cameras changed its direction and fell suddenly to the floor. The other two cameras stopped for a second and he saw that Veronica had tripped and fallen. Behind her, he caught the briefest possible glimpse of the thing that was chasing them, but before he could get a good look at it, both Lynne and Brad turned back and starting running, too terrified by what they saw to even consider rescuing their fallen associate.

She screamed out to them, but they did not turn back. John watched as her camera gave him another brief look at the creature standing over her. All he saw was a smile. A horrible inhuman smile darkened by rotting, bared teeth covered with blood. Veronica screamed, and the smile grew even wider and a hand shot out toward the camera and the image on the television turned to static. The screaming stopped.

Terrified by what he saw, John turned around and ran out through the trailer's door, but before his feet reached the ground he felt a hand grab him by his chest. It heaved him up into the air and he fell to the earth below with a painful thud. Too dazed to get up, he turned and saw something standing over him in the darkness. As close as he was to it, all he could see before it ripped out his throat was a very unpleasant smile.

* * *

Lynne and Brad refused to even consider looking back as they ran down the asylum's tangled web of upstairs corridors, which were so haphazardly designed that it seemed as though they were caught in a maze. They were looking for a way downstairs, but had yet to find one.

They were both now convinced that something was truly wrong. The fake game they had signed up for had somehow become horribly real. Veronica was dead. John was long gone. They had yet to see a single hint of the crew's presence. It appeared they were alone, save for whatever it was that was chasing them. All they remembered was its smile. They kept on running even as their bodies edged closer and closer to collapse.

Purely by chance, Brad's eye caught sight of a metal chute attached to the wall as the two of them raced down another hallway. He stopped and turned and ran back to it.

"What are you doing?" Lynne hissed at him in a disbelieving whisper.

"This might be a way down," he whispered back. His voice was slowly returning to normal.

The chute was marked GARBAGE and it opened with a shrill squeak. It was just big enough for the two of them to fit.

"But we don't know where it leads," said Lynne.

"It's gotta go to the furnace," Brad told her. "Where else would the garbage go?"

"The furnace? Are you nuts?"

"Don't be stupid," he derided her. "The thing hasn't been lit for close to a century."

In the distance they heard the sound of heavy, rapid footsteps.

Lynn climbed into the chute and was quickly followed by Brad. They slid down for what seemed like a long time before their ride ended suddenly. They landed on something soft, or at least something softer than they were expecting. The inside of the furnace was huge, big enough to be mistaken for a small room or a large closet. It had to be to heat a building as large as Cravenhearst.

Both Lynne and Brad had to wait a minute before their minds were ready to process where they were. The first thing they noticed was the cause of their soft landing. They were not alone. The furnace was filled with people, none of whom were fortunate enough to still be alive. Lynne started to scream as Brad began to desperately search for a way out. All he found were John and Veronica, and both of them were far too dead to appreciate the reunion. He also found Lorraine and Darren and Chip and a bunch of other people he didn't recognize.

As he scrambled, he heard something happening outside of the furnace.

"Shut up!" he hissed angrily at his hysterical companion.

Startled, Lynne stopped screaming. She too heard the sounds outside. "What is that?" she asked. "What's going on?"

From beneath one of the corpses, Brad spotted a small glimmer of light. He pushed the body out of the way and looked through the small hole. All he saw were dark creatures with large, unnerving smiles.

"That issss the lasssst of them," one of them said, its words bubbling and frothing inside of its throat.

The other creature nodded and moved out of Brad's sight, but he heard it as it started bringing the furnace back to life.

Brad, realizing what was happening, began to scream and started pounding against the furnace's metal wall. Lynne joined him as the smell of gas began to fill in the space around them.

Their screams continued as a small spark erupted and the gas exploded around them into a wall of fire. And then their screams ended and there was only silence.

"Yesssss." One of the creatures nodded as the furnace's warmth reached his cold dead body, causing his smile to grow even wider. "That issss better."

"The hosssspital will warm and the othersss will arissse," said the other one.

"It isss going to be a good day."

As the two of them waited for their friends to join them, the sky outside began to glow with the early glimmer of morning dusk.

The sun was coming up. A new day was starting.

The End